DATE DUE

			PRINTED IN U.S.A.

OPPOSING
VIEWPOINTS®
SERIES

The Millennial Generation

Other Books of Related Interest

Opposing Viewpoints Series

Social Security

At Issue Series

What is the Future of the US Economy?

Current Controversies Series

The Global Impact of Social Media

"Congress shall make no law ... abridging the freedom of speech, or of the press."

First Amendment to the US Constitution

The basic foundation of our democracy is the First Amendment guarantee of freedom of expression. The Opposing Viewpoints Series is dedicated to the concept of this basic freedom and the idea that it is more important to practice it than to enshrine it.

OPPOSING
VIEWPOINTS®
SERIES

The Millennial Generation

David Haugen and Susan Musser, Book Editors

GREENHAVEN PRESS
A part of Gale, Cengage Learning

GALE
CENGAGE Learning®

Detroit • New York • San Francisco • New Haven, Conn • Waterville, Maine • London

GALE
CENGAGE Learning

Elizabeth Des Chenes, *Director, Publishing Solutions*

For more information, contact:
Greenhaven Press
27500 Drake Rd.
Farmington Hills, MI 48331-3535
Or you can visit our Internet site at gale.cengage.com.

For product information and technology assistance, contact us at:

Gale Customer Support, 1-800-877-4253.
For permission to use material from this text or product, submit all requests online at www.cengage.com/permissions.

Further permissions questions can be emailed to permissionrequest@cengage.com.

Articles in Greenhaven Press anthologies are often edited for length to meet page requirements. In addition, original titles of these works are changed to clearly present the main thesis and to explicitly indicate the author's opinion. Every effort is made to ensure that Greenhaven Press accurately reflects the original intent of the authors. Every effort has been made to trace the owners of copyrighted material.

Cover Image © JGI/Tom Grill/Blend Images/Corbis.

LIBRARY OF CONGRESS CATALOGING-IN-PUBLICATION DATA

The millennial generation / David Haugen and Susan Musser, book editors.
    p. cm. -- (Opposing viewpoints)
  Includes bibliographical references and index.
    ISBN 978-0-7377-6326-3 (hbk.) -- ISBN 978-0-7377-6327-0 (pbk.)
  1. Generation Y--Juvenile literature. 2. Youth--Social conditions--21st century--Juvenile literature. 3. Generations--Juvenile literature. I. Haugen, David M., 1969- II. Musser, Susan.
  HQ799.5.M55 2012
  305.235--dc23

                          2012008677

Printed in the United States of America
1 2 3 4 5 6 7 16 15 14 13 12

Contents

Chapter 2: How Motivated and Well Educated Is the Millennial Generation?

Chapter 3: What Social Factors Have Shaped the Millennial Generation?

Why Consider Opposing Viewpoints?

> "The only way in which a human being
> can make some approach to knowing
> the whole of a subject is by hearing
> what can be said about it by persons of
> every variety of opinion and studying
> all modes in which it can be looked at
> by every character of mind. No wise
> man ever acquired his wisdom in any
> mode but this."
>
> *John Stuart Mill*

In our media-intensive culture it is not difficult to find differing opinions. Thousands of newspapers and magazines and dozens of radio and television talk shows resound with differing points of view. The difficulty lies in deciding which opinion to agree with and which "experts" seem the most credible. The more inundated we become with differing opinions and claims, the more essential it is to hone critical reading and thinking skills to evaluate these ideas. Opposing Viewpoints books address this problem directly by presenting stimulating debates that can be used to enhance and teach these skills. The varied opinions contained in each book examine many different aspects of a single issue. While examining these conveniently edited opposing views, readers can develop critical thinking skills such as the ability to compare and contrast authors' credibility, facts, argumentation styles, use of persuasive techniques, and other stylistic tools. In short, the Opposing Viewpoints Series is an ideal way to attain the higher-level thinking and reading skills so essential in a culture of diverse and contradictory opinions.

In addition to providing a tool for critical thinking, Opposing Viewpoints books challenge readers to question their own strongly held opinions and assumptions. Most people form their opinions on the basis of upbringing, peer pressure, and personal, cultural, or professional bias. By reading carefully balanced opposing views, readers must directly confront new ideas as well as the opinions of those with whom they disagree. This is not to argue simplistically that everyone who reads opposing views will—or should—change his or her opinion. Instead, the series enhances readers' understanding of their own views by encouraging confrontation with opposing ideas. Careful examination of others' views can lead to the readers' understanding of the logical inconsistencies in their own opinions, perspective on why they hold an opinion, and the consideration of the possibility that their opinion requires further evaluation.

Evaluating Other Opinions

To ensure that this type of examination occurs, Opposing Viewpoints books present all types of opinions. Prominent spokespeople on different sides of each issue as well as well-known professionals from many disciplines challenge the reader. An additional goal of the series is to provide a forum for other, less known, or even unpopular viewpoints. The opinion of an ordinary person who has had to make the decision to cut off life support from a terminally ill relative, for example, may be just as valuable and provide just as much insight as a medical ethicist's professional opinion. The editors have two additional purposes in including these less known views. One, the editors encourage readers to respect others' opinions—even when not enhanced by professional credibility. It is only by reading or listening to and objectively evaluating others' ideas that one can determine whether they are worthy of consideration. Two, the inclusion of such viewpoints encourages the important critical thinking skill of objectively evaluating an author's credentials and bias. This evaluation will illuminate an author's reasons for taking a particular stance on an issue and will aid in readers' evaluation of the author's ideas.

It is our hope that these books will give readers a deeper understanding of the issues debated and an appreciation of the complexity of even seemingly simple issues when good and honest people disagree. This awareness is particularly important in a democratic society such as ours in which people enter into public debate to determine the common good. Those with whom one disagrees should not be regarded as enemies but rather as people whose views deserve careful examination and may shed light on one's own.

Thomas Jefferson once said that "difference of opinion leads to inquiry, and inquiry to truth." Jefferson, a broadly educated man, argued that "if a nation expects to be ignorant and free . . . it expects what never was and never will be." As individuals and as a nation, it is imperative that we consider the opinions of others and examine them with skill and discernment. The Opposing Viewpoints Series is intended to help readers achieve this goal.

David L. Bender and Bruno Leone,
Founders

Introduction

The Millennial generation has been called by many names: Generation M, Generation Y, the Net Generation, the iGen-eration, and Generation Next. The variety of tags reflects the numerous ways in which the media, politicians, social critics, and demographers have defined this generation of young people. Perhaps the most indistinct label "Generation Y" is simply a placeholder, chosen because Generation Y follows Generation X, those people born sometime between the 1960s and early 1980s. The Millennials defined in this way are young people who have birthdays that hover between the 1980s and the turn of the millennium (though each observer seems to hold his or her own precise range of dates).

Alternatively, terms such as the Net Generation and the iGeneration bespeak this global demographic's facility with technology, especially its presumed mastery of communication technologies and the Internet. The name iGeneration is often reserved for those individuals born after the Internet gained wide public use in the 1990s, thus singling out this slice of the global population as people who have never known a world without the World Wide Web. Even the seemingly universal "Generation Next" suggests that this collective will shape a world enhanced by even more astounding technological breakthroughs as well as changes in environmental practices, geopolitics, economies, and cultural interrelations. Whatever name is applied, however, the intention is almost always to show how distinct this generation will be from those that have come before it.

Historians Neil Howe and William Strauss, in their 2000 book *Millennials Rising: The Next Great Generation*, trumpet this generation's uniqueness as a truly positive force. Writing about the qualities of Generation Y in the United States, Howe and Strauss claim, "As a group, Millennials are unlike any other youth generation in living memory. They are more numerous, more affluent, better educated, and more ethnically diverse. More important, they are beginning to manifest a wide array of positive social habits that older Americans no longer associate with youth, including a new focus on teamwork, achievement, modesty, and good conduct. Only a few years from now, this can-do revolution will overwhelm the cynics and pessimists." These authors believe that Millennials were raised with good values—including tolerance and an eagerness to help others—that will translate into an ability to triumph over adversity and reshape the world for the better. Millennials even have their own website, The Next Great Generation, that projects this "can-do" confidence and reveals a connection to issues that range from marketing and fashion to media and politics.

Some critics, however, view the Millennials' confidence as excessive self-interest. In a widely referenced CBS *60 Minutes* segment from November 2007, correspondent Morley Safer found that businesses were fearful of hiring Millennials because they had their own priorities that seemed to trump work duties. For example, according to employers, the new crop of young workers liked to set their own hours and put personal engagements before all others. In a follow-up report on May 23, 2008, CBS writers concluded, "Their priorities are simple: they come first." In addition, one employment consultant interviewed for the piece argued that years of coddling had made Millennial workers expect nothing but rewards and praise for their efforts. She maintained that this generation needs to be "coached" rather than "bossed," warning that businesses would have to change their methods if they hoped to retain young employees. Other commentators have pinned this supposed self-absorption on the array of personal gadgetry and online social network sites that encourage users to express themselves and broadcast their lives as if every moment were significant. In her 2009 book, *The Narcissism Epidemic*, psychology professor Jean Twenge accused young people of using Facebook, MySpace, and YouTube as venues for shameless self-promotion rather than for meaningful sharing, connectivity, and creativity.

Whether the Millennial generation is really "Generation Me" as Twenge contends, is still a subject of debate. Millennials resist such labeling, while older generations tend to want an explanation for why young people seem so different. Such generational conflicts, though, have been around forever. Baby Boomers were criticized for their anti-authoritarianism and their embrace of rebellious rock and roll. Members of Generation X were termed "slackers." Broadly categorizing generations homogenizes individualism and makes one group appear radically different than another. Kali H. Trzesniewski, a psychology professor at the University of Western Ontario, and M. Brent Donnellan, a psychology professor from Michigan State University, published a report in 2010 that surveyed high-school seniors from 1976 to 2006 and gathered data on their sense of egotism, life satisfaction, reaction to authorities, political activity, and other habits and attitudes. The authors concluded that the "study cast considerable doubt on the idea that there is anything singular about the generation born in the 1970s, 1980s, and 1990s." According to Donnellan, as quoted on the website Gimundo, "Kids these days are about the same as they were back in the mid-1970s."

In *Opposing Viewpoints: The Millennial Generation*, various experts offer their opinions on the singularity of Generation Y. In the first two chapters titled What Defines the Millennial Generation? and How Motivated and Well Educated Is the Millennial Generation?, commentators debate the proposed traits of the Millennials and whether these characteristics are affecting their performance in the workplace and academia. The last two chapters—What Social Factors Have Shaped the Millennial Generation? and How Will the Millennial Generation Impact the Future?—bring together analysts who examine this generation on a grand scale. The authors in these final chapters debate what legacy the Millennials are likely to leave behind. Overall, the writers in the following chapters paint a picture of a generation that is easier to pin down in terms of birth date than shared attitudes. Certainly, the Millennials have grown up in a digital world, but it remains a subject of conjecture whether this reality has shaped a new breed of young people or simply another generation is taking advantage of innovation and building a world that will cater to its needs and desires.

CHAPTER 1

What Defines the Millennial Generation?

Chapter Preface

The Millennial generation is commonly defined by a list of shared traits as well as by a specific range of birth dates. Taking cues from various polls, most observers claim members of the Millennial generation are dedicated users of digital technologies such as smart phones, portable computer tablets, and mp3 music players. They are also skilled in surfing the Internet and deeply connected to social networking sites such as Facebook and Twitter, sharing thoughts and feelings freely in online forums and public chat rooms. Some, like psychology professor and author Jean Twenge, argue that the concern with broadcasting oneself is a sign that the Millennials are too self-absorbed, but others have insisted that Generation Y has shown more progressive thinking and concern for others than previous generations. Authors Morley Winograd and Michael D. Hais assert in a July 31, 2009 article on NewGeography.com that "Millennials are very much concerned about and connected to the world around them—more so, in fact, than many older Americans." Winograd and Hais contend that digital communication and social networking has, in fact, allowed Millennials to reach out to people across the globe, facilitating cross-cultural contacts and helping to end divisive stereotyping.

Winograd and Hais are also convinced that young people in the United States are connected to both local and national issues. They report that Millennials are volunteering in record numbers, having been taught that "the best way to solve a societal problem is to act upon it locally and directly." By banding together both in person and online, young people recognize the power of united action, these authors insist. They point to the election of President Barack Obama as the prime example of how collective action from an unprecedented number of young voters swayed US politics.

However, not everyone believes Generation Y is a collection of global activists ready to break with the past and unify the world. Peter W. Singer, director of Brookings Institution's 21st Century Defense Initiative, says in a March 2011 CNN interview that a Brookings poll of one thousand young leaders in the United States draws a different picture. Singer says the poll shows that 60 percent of Millennials agree that their own political views are mostly influenced by their parents. In addition, the Brookings survey found that 58 percent of the young leaders "think that America is 'too involved' in global affairs and should instead focus more on issues at home."

Instead of defining Millennials as global citizens, Singer argues the data suggests that future US leaders are isolationists. Of course, even as Singer admits, the attitudes expressed in opinion polls are not "set in stone." As the debates in this chapter attest, survey data can be interpreted in often contradictory ways. Nevertheless, analysts, politicians, and media pundits continue their attempts to define the Millennial generation, seeking to better understand them by their actions and professed beliefs and hoping to predict how this generation will impact global relations, national politics, and the economy today and tomorrow.

> *"To critics, this generation is an army of self-absorbed narcissists with a swollen sense of entitlement"*

Have We Raised a Generation of Narcissists?

Steve Chapman

Much of the debate about the current generation of young people has characterized them by their technological savvy and labeled them Generation Y or the Millennials; however, Jean Twenge offers a different take on and label for this group. Twenge argues that this generation is more self-involved than previous generations, and that this defining trait not only guides their decision-making and actions, but also permeates the culture in which they live. In the following viewpoint, Steve Chapman argues that although the Millennial generation is self-absorbed, they seem to be doing just fine. Steve Chapman is a columnist for the Chicago Tribune.

As you read, consider the following questions:

1. Who is Jean Twenge?
2. What negative comments were made about the parents of the Millennial generation?

3. According to the article, how have the members of
Generation Y coped with high expectations?

Growing older has many drawbacks and one unalloyed pleasure: passing judgment on the younger generation. Lately,
people have been scrutinizing the members of Generation Y and
finding them deficient.

What's wrong with the kids? A recent article in *The Wall
Street Journal* reported that because they have been told since
infancy that they were special, they believe it and expect to keep
hearing it. "Bosses, professors and mates are feeling the need to
lavish praise on young adults, particularly twentysomethings,
or else see them wither under an unfamiliar compliment defi-
cit," it said.

Self-Absorbed Narcissists

To critics, this generation is an army of self-absorbed narcissists
with a swollen sense of entitlement. In my house, I have tried to
prevent this outcome by reminding my kids, "The world does
not revolve around you. It revolves around me." But apparently
some parents didn't dispense that wisdom.

Jean Twenge, an associate professor of psychology at San
Diego State University, reports that college students increasingly
agree with statements indicating oversized egos, such as "I am an
important person." Marian Salzman, a senior vice president at
the advertising agency JWT, told *The Christian Science Monitor*,
"Gen-Y is the most difficult workforce I've ever encountered,"
because they "are so self-indulgent."

But before Gen Y-ers start to feel bad about themselves, they
should know that worse things were said about their parents.
Back in the 1960s and '70s, it was universal wisdom that the
kids of that era suffered from too much coddling. Vice President
Spiro Agnew blamed student unrest and other problems on
"spoiled brats who never had a good spanking." Best-selling author Norman Vincent Peale, author of "The Power of Positive

Adults Encourage Youths' Delusions

Ann Hulbert, the dean of the history of American childhood, has pointed out that the adults who have been so eager to legitimize emerging adulthood [a proposed developmental stage between childhood and adulthood characterized by the search for self] do not "seem to be asking themselves whether fixating on the phase will help twentysomethings outgrow it." In a response in *Slate* to the [*New York Times* Robin Marantz] Henig piece, she wrote, [psychologist Jeffrey Jensen] "Arnett's new category perhaps says more about how parental figures think about young people than about how young people think about themselves (unless they've by now swallowed their elders' theories)." What Henig and Arnett and their supporters have overlooked is the possibility that young people have in fact modeled themselves on their elders' theories, and that the well-meaning army of parents and nonprofit administrators enlisted to support their self-explorations and self-realizations are merely exacerbating a delusion.

Rita Koganzon, "Slacking as Self-Discovery," New Atlantis: A Journal of Technology and Society, *Fall 2010.*

Thinking," complained about youngsters whose parents felt a duty to "satisfy their every desire."

It's a hoot to hear modern kids described as self-indulgent by the generation that created its own culture out of sex, drugs and rock 'n' roll. Talk about a sense of entitlement: When the baby boomers came along, they (we) got the voting age lowered for their benefit. They also demanded that the drinking age be lowered, and it was—only to be raised once they were safely into adulthood. Narcissism? Not for nothing were boomers dubbed the "Me Generation."

Most of the grousing is just what every new crop of kids hears from its elders, who forget that when they were young, they were equally infuriating. People who came of age during the Great Depression and World War II are known as the "Greatest Generation," but their parents didn't call them that when they were going through puberty. *Bye Bye Birdie*, the musical that asked the question "What's the matter with kids these days?," debuted during the Eisenhower administration.

High Expectations

The young people we accuse of being hopelessly self-satisfied are the same ones who have been told they had to score high on the SAT, get straight A's and cure cancer just to get into a decent college. Far from being hothouse flowers who wilt under pressure, they've coped with high expectations and intense competition.

This year, Harvard accepted only 9 percent of undergraduate applicants, the lowest figure in its history, down from 18 percent in 1983. The same trend is evident at other selective schools.

You would think the epidemic of narcissism would translate into selfish, destructive conduct. But on most counts, today's youngsters comport themselves more responsibly than Mom and Dad did at their age.

In 1977, 29 percent of high-school seniors smoked cigarettes daily. By 2006, only 12 percent did. The number of high-school seniors who regularly use illicit drugs declined by 43 percent during that period, while the number who regularly consume alcohol dropped by more than a third.

Over the last quarter-century, the juvenile arrest rate has fallen as well. Teenage girls are far less likely today than before to get pregnant or to have abortions.

Maybe all that self-esteem has led modern youngsters to the conclusion that their lives and bodies are far too valuable to risk on reckless behavior. Maybe when they hold a high opinion of themselves, it's because they've earned it through diligence and self-restraint.

From all objective indicators, this generation is doing just fine. And if all they need to keep doing it is a steady supply of praise, I say give it to them.

> *"The widespread negative portrayals of today's generation of young Americans are not based on trustworthy evidence that they actually are worse than the young Americans of 30 years ago."*

Members of the Millennial Generation Are Not More Self-Absorbed than Previous Generations

Jeffrey Jensen Arnett

As members of the Millennial generation have grown into adults, many scholars and commentators have bemoaned the characteristics they see as typical of this generation, especially their narcissism. However, in the viewpoint that follows, Jeffrey Jensen Arnett contends that this generation of young Americans is no more self-centered than previous generations. Arnett counters the critics by explaining the self-focus as a corollary of a new life stage—emerging adulthood—situated between childhood and adulthood, during

Jeffrey Jensen Arnett, "Oh, Grow Up! Generational Grumbling and the New Life Stage of Emerging Adulthood—Commentary on Trzesniewski & Donnellan," *Perspectives on Psychological Science*, vol. 5, no. 1, 2010, pp. 89–92. Copyright © 2010 by Sage Publications, Inc. All rights reserved. Reproduced by permission.

which individuals explore their identity and life possibilities, but eventually move past to become well-adjusted adults who contribute to society. Arnett is a developmental psychologist at Clark University and author of numerous books on emerging adulthood including Emerging Adulthood: The Winding Road from the Late Teens through the Twenties.

As you read, consider the following questions:

1. As stated by the author, what are the four main reasons why adults view emerging adults negatively?
2. What feature has Arnett suggested as being "developmentally distinctive about emerging adulthood"?
3. What does the author identify as the dreams of emerging adults?

Is there any basis for the widespread negative portrayal of today's young Americans as selfish, suffering slackers? Or is this a myth promoted by irresponsible researchers and hyped by credulous journalists? In their article "Rethinking 'Generation Me': A Study of Cohort Effects From 1976–2006," [psychologist Kali H.] Trzesniewski and [psychologist Brent] Donnellan . . . do a masterful job of presenting data that provide a definitive answer to these questions. The data show unambiguously that the claims made by [psychologist Jean] Twenge and others are grossly exaggerated. American high-school seniors in the early 21st century are remarkably similar to their counterparts in the late 1970s. Despite many complaints about the decline of young people and their sorry state today, it turns out that the high-school seniors of 2006 are no different from the high-school seniors of 1976 on a wide range of variables, from self-esteem and life satisfaction to loneliness and antisocial behavior. Hopefully, the careful, thorough analysis in this article will drive a stake through the heart of the overhyped claims of Generation Me.

Trzesniewski and Donnellan have done their work well, and I have little to quarrel with in their cogent, comprehensive analysis. Instead, I will focus my remarks here on the interesting issue they raise at the end of their article: "Perhaps the more interesting psychological story concerns the persistence of beliefs about cohort-related changes when clear evidence of such effects is fairly limited and the positive effect sizes are small by psychological standards". If so little evidence supports the claim that today's young people are worse in multiple ways than young people of a few decades ago, why is this claim so widely embraced?

The Rise of Emerging Adulthood

Trzesniewski and Donnellan present a variety of good answers to this question themselves, but I wish to offer an additional answer that I think goes beyond what they offered. The reason young people in American society are perceived so negatively is not because high-school seniors in the early 21st century are much different from high-school seniors of the late 1970s, but because the period beyond high school really has changed dramatically over this time. Instead of entering adult roles of marriage, parenthood, and stable work shortly after high school, as most young people did in 1976, today most wait until at least their late 20s to make these transitions. Instead of going directly from adolescence to young adulthood, most now experience a new life stage, emerging adulthood, from their late teens to at least their mid-20s.

Why would the rise of emerging adulthood as a normative life stage provoke grumbling about young people in this age period? I believe there are four main reasons: (a) the later entrance into adult roles by today's emerging adults is misinterpreted by older adults as selfishness, (b) the identity explorations of emerging adulthood are misinterpreted as widespread suffering, (c) the search by emerging adults for identity-based work leads older adults to see them as slackers uninterested in "real" work, and

(d) their high hopes for their lives are misinterpreted by others as grandiosity. Here I will explain why each of these beliefs about emerging adults is mistaken.

Self-Focused Is Not the Same as Selfish

Changes in the timing of entering adult roles have been rapid and dramatic over the past three decades. In 1976, the year Trzesniewski and Donnellan begin their analysis, the median marriage age in the United States was between 22 and 23 years old. By 2006, the last year in their analysis, the median marriage age had risen to nearly 27 [according to the US Bureau of the Census], an increase of more than 4 years in just three decades. College participation also rose, especially for women. From 1976 to 2006, [the National Center for Education Statistics found that] the number of young women entering college after high school doubled, and by 2006 two thirds of women entered college after high school and 57% of American undergraduates were female. College participation among young men also rose during this interval, although less dramatically.

One consequence of these changes, lightning fast in historical terms, was the opening up of the new life stage of emerging adulthood between adolescence and young adulthood. The rise of this new life stage has taken place so quickly that many people find it disconcerting, which causes them to view emerging adults negatively. The parents and grandparents of today's emerging adults may be tempted to apply the norms of their time to their progeny. "By the time I was 23," they may think, "I was married, had a child on the way, and had been working in a stable job for 5 years. Yet these kids are around that age now and seem nowhere near any of those transitions. What's wrong with them? Why are they so selfish?"

But seeing them as selfish is a consequence of applying obsolete norms to the present and of an unjustifiably negative view of the characteristics of the new life stage of emerging adulthood. One of the features I have proposed as developmentally distinctive about emerging adulthood is the *self-focused age* meaning that is the time of life in which there is the least social control from binding relationships and the greatest scope for making independent decisions. But this does not mean they are selfish. On the contrary, [human development professor William Aquilino has argued that] they tend to be considerably less ego-centric than adolescents and much better at taking others' per-spective, most notably their parents'. They are self-focused during emerging adulthood because they are immersed in their identity explorations and on building the skills they will need for adult life. Also, they realize—wisely—that they have freedom for self-directed action in their 20s that they never had as children or ado-lescents and that they will probably never have again in adulthood. They neither expect nor desire to be self-focused forever, and the great majority have entered adult commitments of long-term work, marriage or other partnership, and parenthood by age 30.

Emerging Adults Are Exploring Their Identity

The second reason for the negative view of emerging adults is that their identity explorations may be interpreted as suffering. Identity issues may once have been the primary developmental challenge of adolescence, as [psychologist Erik] Erikson pro-posed over a half century ago. However, in the early 21st cen-tury, it is during emerging adulthood, not adolescence, that most young people in industrialized countries explore the op-tions available to them in love and work and move toward mak-ing enduring choices. Identity explorations can be exciting and fun, but they can also be disorienting and confusing and are sometimes seen as suffering rather than as a normal part of the identity challenges of the age. This is true not only among older adults, but even among some emerging adults themselves, as the popularity of the "quarterlife crisis" idea attests [as in Alexandra Robbins and Abby Wilner's book *Quarterlife Crisis: The Unique Challenges of Life in Your Twenties*].

Parents' Actions Contribute to Emerging Adulthood

The "changing timetable for adulthood" has, in many ways, become internalized by 20-somethings and their parents alike. Today young people don't expect to marry until their late 20s, don't expect to start a family until their 30s, don't expect to be on track for a rewarding career until much later than their parents were. So they make decisions about their futures that reflect this wider time horizon. Many of them would not be ready to take on the trappings of adulthood any earlier even if the opportunity arose; they haven't braced themselves for it.

Nor do parents expect their children to grow up right away—and they might not even want them to. Parents might regret having themselves jumped into marriage or a career and hope for more considered choices for their children. Or they might want to hold on to a reassuring connection with their children as the kids leave home. If they were "helicopter parents"—a term that describes heavily invested parents who hover over their children, swooping down to take charge and solve problems at a moment's notice—they might keep hovering and problem-solving long past the time when their children should be solving problems on their own. This might, in a strange way, be part of what keeps their grown children in the limbo between adolescence and adulthood. It can be hard sometimes to tease out to what extent a child doesn't quite want to grow up and to what extent a parent doesn't quite want to let go.

Robin Marantz Henig, "What Is It About 20-Somethings?," New York Times Magazine, *August 18, 2010.*

However, it is notable that numerous studies find that well-being, self-esteem, and life satisfaction all rise steadily over the course of emerging adulthood for most people. For a small proportion of emerging adults, serious psychopathology such as major depression increases in the 20s but most people appear to experience the identity challenges of the age as more exhilarating than onerous.

Young Employees Are Asserting Their Interests over Employers

A third reason for the negative view of emerging adults is their high expectations for work. They expect work to be not just a job but an adventure, not just a way to put bread on the table and a roof over their heads but a venue for self-development and self-expression. In short, they expect their work to be identity-based and something that provides a satisfying fit with their assessment of their talents and interests.

How dare they! This seems to be the reaction of many employers and other adults to emerging adults' aspirations. Don't they know that work is supposed to be drudgery, something that employees are supposed to submit to at the behest of employers, preferably while keeping their mouths shut? Evidently, however, emerging adults appear not to have received that memo. Having grown up in a time of great affluence and economic vitality, today's emerging adults expect work to be enjoyable, and if the job they have fails to please them, they move on before long, unencumbered as they are by the responsibilities of providing for anyone but themselves. Perhaps this is indeed selfish of them, but it could also be seen as a long-overdue assertion of the interests of employees against the interests of employers.

Optimism Should Not Be Denigrated

Finally, one other reason for negative views of today's emerging adults is their high hopes for the future or what Twenge calls their "narcissism." I have found that high hopes in emerging adulthood are remarkably widespread. Across ethnic groups and social classes, American emerging adults almost universally believe that eventually life will be kind to them. Even if life is not going so well right now—and often it is not, what with job changes, love upheavals, and financial difficulties—eventually all will be well. Everyone will find a job that provides a satisfying identity fit, pays well, and maybe even does some good in the world. Everyone will eventually find not just a mere flesh and blood marriage partner but a "soul mate."

Is this a new narcissism, or just the enduring hopefulness of youth, who have not yet had their dreams tested in the fires of reality? Trzesniewski and Donnellan find no evidence that self-assessments of intellectual abilities relative to peers have changed over the past 30 years. They did find that expectations for educational attainment have increased, but—and this is my one criticism of their article—they are too quick to concede that today's American high-school seniors "have higher and perhaps unrealistic expectations for their future". Actually, the high-school seniors' expectations are not unrealistic but a recognition of the fact that as a group they will certainly have higher educational attainment than their peers did 30 years ago. Furthermore, as Trzesniewski and Donnellan note later in their article, it is in fact highly realistic of them to recognize the changes in the American economy over the past 30 years from manufacturing to information and technology. It would, in fact, be dangerously unrealistic not to respond to the increasing economic reward for obtaining postsecondary education and the increasing penalty for failing to do so.

Emerging adults today have high hopes, but it is hard to see why they should be denigrated for that. Few aspire to be professional sports heroes, musical superstars, or Hollywood icons, as adolescents often do. Their dreams are simpler: just the right job, and just the right love partner, and enough money to live well. Even as they strive for these simple dreams, they stay connected to the real options their lives present. I have found that, as they approach 30, they adjust their dreams without trauma to the exigencies of reality.

Emerging Adulthood Is a New Life Stage

In sum, the widespread negative portrayals of today's generation of young Americans are not based on trustworthy evidence that they actually are worse than the young Americans of 30 years ago. Instead, the main reason for portraying them negatively is that the life stage of emerging adulthood has grown up in between adolescence and young adulthood so rapidly that many people still not have adjusted their expectations to the new norm.

With the passage of years, it may be that emerging adulthood will come to be expected as a normative life stage, especially as more people who have experienced emerging adulthood become parents and grandparents themselves. Perhaps emerging adulthood will even come to be widely valued for the possibilities it offers for identity explorations in pursuit of ideals in love and work.

What seems certain is that emerging adulthood is not merely a generational phenomenon that will be gone in another 20 or 30 years, but a new life stage that will be normative in industrialized societies for the foreseeable future and increasingly in developing countries as well. Widespread postsecondary education, marriage and parenthood in late 20s or beyond, the search for a soul mate and identity-based work—none of these are likely to be reversed in the decades to come. Generations—and glib generational generalizations—may come and go, but emerging adulthood is here to stay.

*"Those who were born digital don't
remember a world in which letters
were printed and sent . . . or where
people met up at formal dances
rather than on Facebook."*

Born Digital: Understanding the First Generation of Digital Natives

John Palfrey and Urs Gasser

*In the viewpoint that follows, John Palfrey and Urs Gasser intro-
duce the concept of digital natives and argue that young Americans can be defined by traits typical of this group. Most common
among these characteristics is the tendency to live the majority of
one's life with most social interaction, information retrieval, and
sharing occurring in the online realm. Unlike individuals of previous generations who have had to adjust to a world dominated by
digital technologies, the authors contend that digital natives feel
comfortable living their lives online and have readily incorporated
new forms of communication, such as e-mail and social networking, into their daily lives. While Palfrey and Gasser believe digital
natives have the capacity to use digital technologies to bring about
positive change, they remain cautious about the possibly negative*

outcomes that could develop if certain tendencies of this group, such as disregard for privacy, continue unabated. Palfrey is a professor of law and vice dean of Harvard Law School, and Gasser is an associate professor of law at the University of St. Gallen. Both have written about and extensively researched the relationship between the Internet and society.

As you read, consider the following questions:

1. As stated by the authors, what are the differences between "digital settlers," "digital immigrants," and "digital natives"?
2. What are some of the common practices of digital natives, according to Palfrey and Gasser?
3. What contrasts do the authors point out between digital natives' research practices and those of previous generations?

You see them everywhere. The teenage girl with the iPod, sitting across from you on the subway, frenetically typing messages into her cell phone. The whiz kid summer intern in your office who knows what to do when your e-mail client crashes. The eight-year-old who can beat you at any video game on the market—and types faster than you do, too. Even your niece's newborn baby in London, whom you've never met, but with whom you have bonded nonetheless, owing to the new batch of baby photos that arrive each week.

All of them are "Digital Natives." They were all born after 1980, when social digital technologies, such as Usenet and bulletin board systems, came online. They all have access to networked digital technologies. And they all have the skills to use those technologies. (Except for the baby—but she'll learn soon enough.) . . .

These kids are different. They study, work, write, and interact with each other in ways that are very different from the ways that you did growing up. They read blogs rather than newspapers. They often meet each other online before they meet in person. They probably don't even know what a library card looks like, much less have one; and if they do, they've probably never used it. They get their music online—often for free, illegally—rather than buying it in record stores. They're more likely to send an instant message (IM) than to pick up the telephone to arrange a date later in the afternoon. They adopt and pal around with virtual Neopets online instead of pound puppies. And they're connected to one another by a common culture. Major aspects of their lives—social interactions, friendships, civic activities—are mediated by digital technologies. And they've never known any other way of life.

Beginning in the late 1970s, the world began to change—and fast. The first online bulletin board system (or "BBS," for short) let people with clunky computer equipment and access to telephone lines swap documents, read news online, and send one another messages. Usenet groups, organized around topics of interest to communities of users, became popular in the early 1980s. E-mail began to enter popular usage later in the 1980s. The World Wide Web made its debut in 1991, with easy-to-use browsers widely accessible a few years later. Search engines, portals, and e-commerce sites hit the scene in the late 1990s. By the turn of the millennium, the first social networks and blogs cropped up online. In 2001, Polaroid declared bankruptcy, just as sales of digital cameras started to take off. In 2006, Tower Records liquidated its stores; by 2008, iTunes had become the largest music retailer in the United States. Today, most young people in many societies around the world carry mobile devices—cell phones, Sidekicks, iPhones—at all times, and these devices don't just make phone calls; they also send text messages, surf the Internet, and download music.

This is the most rapid period of technological transformation ever, at least when it comes to information. The Chinese invented the printing press several *centuries* before Johannes Gutenberg developed the European printing press in the mid-1400s and churned out his first Bibles. Few people could afford the printed books made possible by presses for another several centuries. By contrast, the invention and adoption of digital technologies by more than a billion people worldwide has occurred over the span of a few decades. Despite the saturation of digital technologies in many cultures, no generation has yet lived from cradle to grave in the digital era.

No major aspect of modern life is untouched by the way many of us now use information technologies. Business, for instance, can be done more quickly and over greater distances, often with much less capital required to get up and running. Politicians e-mail their constituents, offer video introductions to their campaigns on their websites, and provide volunteers with sophisticated digital tools to organize events on their own. Even religion is being transformed: Priests and pastors, imams, rabbis, gurus, and even Buddhist monks have begun to reach their faithful through their weblogs.

Most notable, however, is the way the digital era has transformed how people live their lives and relate to one another and to the world around them. Some older people were there at the start, and these "Digital Settlers"—though not native to the digital environment, because they grew up in an analog-only world—have helped to shape its contours. These older people are online, too, and often quite sophisticated in their use of these technologies, but they also continue to rely heavily on traditional, analog forms of interaction. Others less familiar with this environment, "Digital Immigrants," learned how to e-mail and use social networks late in life. You know them by the lame jokes and warnings about urban myths that they still forward to large cc: lists. Those who were born digital don't remember a world in which letters were printed and sent, much less handwritten, or where people met up at formal dances rather than on Facebook. The changing nature of human relationships is second nature to some, and learned behavior to others.

This narrative is about those who wear the earbuds of an iPod on the subway to their first job, not those of us who still remember how to operate a Sony Walkman or remember buying LPs or eight-track tapes. Much is changing beyond just how much young people pay (or don't pay) for their music. The young people becoming university students and new entrants in the workforce, while living much of their lives online, are different from us along many dimensions. Unlike those of us just a shade older, this new generation didn't have to relearn anything to live lives of digital immersion. They learned in digital the first time around; they only know a world that is digital.

Unlike most Digital Immigrants, Digital Natives live much of their lives online, without distinguishing between the online and the offline. Instead of thinking of their digital identity and their real-space identity as separate things, they just have an identity (with representations in two, or three, or more different spaces). They are joined by a set of common practices, including the amount of time they spend using digital technologies, their tendency to multitask, their tendency to express themselves and relate to one another in ways mediated by digital technologies, and their pattern of using the technologies to access and use information and create new knowledge and art forms. For these young people, new digital technologies—computers, cell phones, Sidekicks—are primary mediators of human-to-human connections. They have created a 24/7 network that blends the human with the technical to a degree we haven't experienced before, and it is transforming human relationships in fundamental ways. They feel as comfortable in online spaces as they do in offline ones. They don't think of their hybrid lives as anything remarkable. Digital Natives haven't known anything but a life connected to one another, and to the world of bits, in this manner.

Digital Natives are constantly connected. They have plenty of friends, in real space and in the virtual worlds—indeed, a growing collection of friends they keep a count of, often for the rest of the world to see, in their online social network sites. Even as they sleep, connections are made online, in the background; they wake up to find them each day. Sometimes, these connections are to people the Digital Native would never have had a chance to meet in the offline world. Through social network sites, Digital Natives connect with and IM and share photos with friends all over the world. They may also collaborate creatively or politically in ways that would have been impossible thirty years ago. But in the course of this relentless connectivity, the very nature of relationships—even what it means to "befriend" someone—is changing. Online friendships are based on many of the same things as traditional friendships—shared interests, frequent interaction—but they nonetheless have a very different tenor: They are often fleeting; they are easy to enter into and easy to leave, without so much as a goodbye; and they are also perhaps enduring in ways we have yet to understand.

Digital Natives don't just experience friendship differently from their parents; they also relate to information differently. Consider the way Digital Natives experience music. Not so long ago, teenagers would go to a friend's house to listen to a new record. Or music could signal a shared intimacy: A teenage girl would give her new boyfriend a mixed tape, with song names carefully written onto the cassette lining, to signal her growing affection. Not everything has changed: Digital Natives still listen to copious amounts of music. And they still share lots of music. But the experience is far less likely than before to take place in physical space, with friends hanging out together to listen to a stereo system. The network lets them share music that they each, then, can hear through headphones, walking down the street or in their dorm rooms, mediated by an iPod or the iTunes Music System on their hard drive. The mixed tape has given way to the playlist, shared with friends and strangers alike through social networks online. A generation has come to expect music to be digitally formatted, often free for the taking, and endlessly shareable and portable.

Digital Natives are tremendously creative. It is impossible to say whether they are more or less creative than prior generations, but one thing is certain: They express themselves creatively in ways that are very different from the ways their parents did at their age. Many Digital Natives perceive information to be malleable; it is something they can control and reshape in new and interesting ways. That might mean editing a profile on MySpace or encyclopedia entries on Wikipedia, making a movie or online video, or downloading a hot music track—whether lawfully or not. Whether or not they realize it, they have come to have a degree of control over their cultural environment that is unprecedented. Digital Natives can learn how to use a new software program in a snap. They seemingly can take, upload, and edit pictures to share with friends online in their sleep. Digital Natives, at their most creative, are creating parallel worlds on sites like Second Life. And after they do, they record parts of that world and post a video of it on YouTube (if they live in California) or Dailymotion (if they live in Cannes) in a new art form called "machinima." Digital Natives can rework media, using off-the-shelf computer programs, in ways that would have seemed impossible a few short decades ago.

Digital Natives are coming to rely upon this connected space for virtually all of the information they need to live their lives. Research once meant a trip to a library to paw through a musty card catalog and puzzle over the Dewey Decimal System to find a book to pull off the shelves. Now, research means a Google search—and, for most, a visit to Wikipedia before diving deeper into a topic. They simply open a browser, punch in a search term, and dive away until they find what they want—or what they thought they wanted. Most Digital Natives don't buy the newspaper—ever. It's not that they don't read the news, it's just that they get it in new ways and in a wide variety of formats. And they have little use for those big maps you have to fold on the creases, or for TV listings, travel guides, or pamphlets of any sort; the print versions are not obsolete, but they do strike Digital Natives as rather quaint. These changes, to be sure, are not all good, but they will be enduring.

Indeed, many aspects of the way in which Digital Natives lead their lives are cause for concern. Digital Natives' ideas about privacy, for instance, are different from those of their parents and grandparents. In the process of spending so much time in this digitally connected environment, Digital Natives are leaving more traces of themselves in public places online. At their best, they show off who they aspire to be and put their most creative selves before the world. At their worst, they put information online that may put them in danger, or that could humiliate them in years to come. With every hour they log online, they are leaving more tracks for marketers—and pedophiles, for that matter—to follow. There's more about them for admissions officers and potential employers—and potential dates—to find. The repercussions of these changes, in the decades to come, will be profound for all of us. But those who are growing up as Digital Natives are on track to pay the highest price.

Digital Natives will move markets and transform industries, education, and global politics. The changes they bring about as they move into the workforce could have an immensely positive effect on the world we live in. By and large, the digital revolution has already made this world a better place. And Digital Natives have every chance of propelling society further forward in myriad ways—if we let them.

"Our work should be read as a plea for
further research . . . to dispel the false
dichotomies the Net Generation and
digital native arguments have led to."

Digital Natives Do Not Belong
to Just One Generation

Chris Jones and Laura Czerniewicz

*A large amount of the ongoing discourse concerning the current
generation of youth has defined them by the digital culture and
society in which they have grown up, labeling those born into
this culture "digital natives" and those not born during this time
"digital immigrants." However, in the viewpoint that follows, Chris
Jones and Laura Czerniewicz dispute the tendency to categorize
digital natives and immigrants in generational terms. They argue
that this divide oversimplifies the complex forces at work in de-
termining whether an individual feels comfortable using technologies. While they do not deny that changes are taking place as a
result of peoples' engagement with ever-advancing technological
media, they maintain that the understanding of this phenomenon
is incomplete and must move away from the current generation-
centered debate. Jones is professor at the Institute of Educational
Technology at the Open University in the United Kingdom, and*

Czerniewicz is a professor at the Center for Educational Technology at the University of Cape Town in South Africa.

As you read, consider the following questions:

1. As stated by the authors, what is the "general claim made in the Net Generation and digital natives discourse"?
2. What does the determinism that the authors view as inherent in the "digital natives" debate demand of education and technology?
3. According to the authors, how will the understanding of youths' identities as they relate to technology need to change if the determinist view is abandoned?

The idea that there has been a sharp and fundamental break between young people and previous generations has become commonplace. It can be found widely in policy statements and in commercial rhetoric, it is referenced repeatedly in academic work and it persists despite a growing body of evidence that questions the foundations of the idea. . . .

There is a current and popularized discourse about a new generation of young people who have been 'bathed in bits and bytes' since birth. This discourse has a wide social impact and its echoes can be found in business literature and government policy. The prima facie claim is a powerful one because many of the audience for the idea have some prior experience of young people who have grown up in an environment infused with digital technologies. These young people are not only familiar with a range of new devices but they also grew up with the Internet and the Web. The general claim, made in the Net Generation and digital natives discourse, is that this material context has led to young people developing a natural aptitude and high skill levels in relation to the new technologies. In contrast those older people who grew up in an analogue world are portrayed as always being behind, as being immigrants to the new world. It is suggested that these older digital immigrants are never likely to reach the same levels of skill and fluency that are developed naturally by those who have grown up with the new technologies and the digital native and Net Generation students are said to have particular learning preferences or styles. . . . Even stronger claims are made by some authors [such as Marc Prensky] about changes in the brain occurring as a consequence of exposure to digital technologies.

Overall, the claims made for generational change and the existence of a distinct Net Generation composed of digital natives appears to be a gross oversimplification, and despite the prevalence of the idea of a new generation, there is no consensus on a single term nor is there a commonly agreed start or end date for the new generation. The three most commonly used terms in circulation are the Net Generation, digital natives and Millennials. Among the many other terms that have been used in a similar way are Generation Y and, more recently in response to the current trend in technological and market developments, the i-Generation. Each term for the new generation brings with it some particular characteristic or metaphoric resonance but generally all of the terms are used interchangeably. All these terms suggest that the generational boundary is sharp and that just a few years disparity in age would make a significant difference. The age boundary between the generations varies and a range of dates have been proposed for the new generation despite the claim that the new generation is evidently distinct from previous age cohorts. [Author Don] Tapscott, for example, begins the new generation in January 1977 and ends it with a further generational shift into Generation Next in December 1997. Prensky is not specific about the dates that define this new generation but other authors using the same expression suggest that digital natives appear after 1980. [Diana and James] Oblinger date the Millennials from those born 'in or after 1982' and end the generational cohort in 1991. There remains a need to engage with the Net Generation and digital natives discourse because it continues to have an influence on policy and practice in education, despite the lack of clarity in the use of terms and in the definition of generational boundaries.

The origins of this special edition lie in a 1-day conference held at the Open University (UK) in Milton Keynes during May 2009. That conference brought together the authors of these papers with others working in this field to discuss the work they had been undertaking and to examine the emerging critical commentary on the idea of a Net Generation composed of digital natives. It was followed by a 3-day workshop which focused on the questions that arose from the research, in particular whether the generational idea was exhausted and whether the empirical research that was being reported fatally flawed the idea. Perhaps surprisingly, the group concluded that there was value in further research, firstly because the discourse had a persistence and the source literature was still being referenced in serious academic work, and secondly, because although the idea was flawed it did point to interesting research questions about how digital and networked technologies were being appropriated by students.

Two notable publications had begun to deal with the persistence of the generational divide within academic discourse prior to the workshop. Beyond higher education, there was a more developed discussion that addressed some of the underlying theoretical positions supporting a determinist discourse around technology. Technological determinism is another discourse that has persisted despite a serious academic assault on the basis for the claims that have been made. Technological determinism argues that changes in technology arise independently and that technology then has an impact on other dependant domains in society. The problem that [Donald] MacKenzie and [Judy] Wajcman identify with technological determinism is that it focuses on the need to adapt to technology rather than on how to shape it. In the determinism that is inherent in arguments based on the Net Generation and digital natives, education has to adapt to technologically induced changes rather than shaping the technology-

Experience and Immersion Create Digital Natives

Contrary to the argument put forward by proponents of the digital native concept, generation alone does not adequately define if someone is a digital native or not. . . . It is clear that there are a range of factors involved. It appears that younger people do have a greater range of [information and communication technologies] ICTs in their household, tend to use the Internet as a first port of call, have higher levels of Internet self-efficacy, multi-task more and use the Internet for fact checking and formal learning activities. Nevertheless, generation was not the only significant variable in explaining these activities: gender, education, experience and breadth of use also play a part. Indeed, in all cases immersion in a digital environment (i.e. the breadth of activities that people carry out online) tends to be the most important variable in predicting if someone is a digital native in the way they interact with the technology. . . .

What is very clear is that it is not helpful to define digital natives and immigrants as two distinct, dichotomous generations. While there were differences in how generations engaged with the Internet, there were similarities across generations as well, mainly based on how much experience people have with using technologies. In addition, the findings presented here confirm that individuals' Internet use lies along a continuum of engagement instead of being a dichotomous divide between users and non-users.

Ellen Johanna Helsper and Rebecca Eynon,
"Digital Natives: Where Is the Evidence?"
British Educational Research Journal, *vol. 36,*
no. 3, June 2010.

related changes that are taking place in accordance with educational requirements and the needs of staff and students.

The question of student agency in the process of technology adoption became a central theme in the workshop that took place in 2009. Work had already begun on applying notions of agency found in the work of [Margaret Scott] Archer to this question and during our debates, issues arose about where agency lay in relation to the new technologies being deployed in education. Was agency located at the level of the individual student alone or did agency apply to the collective decisions made in university at the level of departments and whole institutions? What were the conditions within which students made choices about what they could and should do with new technologies, and how did this relate to the notion of technological affordance? . . . If a determinist approach is abandoned then there is a need to develop more nuanced ways of understanding the kinds of identities that young people begin to develop in relation to new technologies. These new understandings will need to connect to the theories that have tried to explain, at a more general level, the kinds of relationships that can help in making sense of education mediation through digital and networked technologies. . . . For example, [Sue] Bennett and [Karl] Maton discuss the idea of networked individualism and [French sociologist Pierre] Bourdieu's interrelated notions of field, capital and habitus. Bourdieu's theoretical constructs are also used to interpret findings [about students' interaction with technology in South Africa] by [Laura] Czerniewicz and [Cheryl] Brown. . . . [Christopher] Jones and [Graham] Healing discuss the place of agency and the relevance of activity theory and actor network theory to this debate. [Gregor] Kennedy *et al.* provide empirically based descriptions of students in the generational age group which suggests that the digital native characteristics can be found, but only among a minority of students. Czerniewicz and Brown provide further empirical evidence from a context in the developing economy of South Africa in which digital networks have yet to become commonplace in education. Even within the South African context, Czerniewicz and Brown find a similar 'elite' group of students to the minority identified by Kennedy *et al.* and they react against the determinist and exclusionary rhetoric that has characterized the debate so far.

Our final comment would be that these papers should not be read as a denial that changes are taking place among young people; indeed we would suggest that our work should be read as a plea for further research to clarify the nature of the changes that are taking place and to dispel the false dichotomies the Net Generation and digital native arguments have led to.

> "Those [twenty-somethings] who do
> secure a job are more likely to switch
> because they're bored or hope to find
> the mythical perfect job."

The Millennial Generation Lacks a Strong Work Ethic

David N. Bass

In the following viewpoint, a twenty-five-year-old conservative writer argues that the Millennial Generation faces difficulties in the workplace because their expectations do not match real-world employment experience and because they have amassed too much education debt. He believes the Millennial Generation expects a large salary in return for "phoned-in job performance." While the Baby Boomers were identified for their strong work ethic, many of the Millennial Generation identify technology use as their strongest identifying marker. David N. Bass is an investigative reporter and associate editor with the John Locke Foundation and CaroIinaJournal.com.

As you read, consider the following questions:

1. What group of people make up the Millennial Generation?

2. What specific costs have risen and therefore prevented the Millennial Generation from reaching financial stability?

3. According to the article, what do 20-somethings do when faced with no job prospects?

Ask anyone above the age of 50 whether "young worker" has become an oxymoron, and they'll say yes. Now, there is hard data to back up the assertion.

Floundering Millennials

In the teeth of the Great Recession, recent college graduates—those in the Millennial generation, born in the 1980s and 1990s—are floundering in a hellish job market. Recent Census figures show that the employment rate among young adults is 55.3 percent, the lowest rate since the end of World War II. One-in-five young adults live in poverty. Teen unemployment stands at 25 percent.

The Associated Press dubs it "the lost generation." But is it really? And if so, who's to blame? Putting aside the media's victim meme, there are many reasons for my generation's predicament (I'm 25), plenty of them a direct result of our own choices.

It's a given that macroeconomic forces beyond the power of an individual are curtailing Millennials' opportunities for financial stability. The job market is flooded with older, more experienced workers jockeying for the same entry-level positions that college graduates desire. The cost of basic needs—groceries, housing, clothing, and gas—has spiked. Wages are stagnant. Due to the federal government's spendthrift ways, my generation faces a debt-saturated future.

Self-Inflicted Wounds

But young people also are lagging because of self-inflicted wounds: Massive student-loan debt, high consumer credit card balances, frequent changing of jobs because of boredom, poor work ethic, entitlement attitudes, heightened standard-of-living expectations, preoccupation with self-esteem, and delay of marriage and parenthood.

Consider: In 2009, the average four-year college graduate owed $24,000 in student-loan debt. That's sustainable if a student leaves school with a degree in a high-demand field—say, nursing or engineering—paying a decent salary right out of the gate. But for liberal arts majors who often spend the first year (if not more) of post-college life waiting tables, it's financial hara-kiri.

It doesn't stop at student loans, though. Graduates leave school, on average, with thousands in credit card debt. Throw in an auto loan, and the debt-to-income ratio goes off the charts. It's tough to get ahead in that financial scenario.

Millennials' Self-Esteem

Do we care? Not really. In fact, the debt burden gives Millennials a self-esteem boost. "Researchers found that the more credit card and college loan debt held by young adults aged 18 to 27, the higher their self-esteem and the more they felt like they were in control of their lives," according to a study published by Ohio State University.

Faced with no job prospects, twenty-somethings often go to graduate school, amassing even more student-loan debt. Those who do secure a job are more likely to switch because they're bored or hope to find the mythical perfect job.

"They have high, unrealistic expectations," Lee Jenkins, a manager partner of Atlanta Capital Group, told *USA Today*. "And many of them don't manage money very well."

In many cases, there is the expectation of a fat salary in exchange for phoned-in job performance—and we're not afraid to admit it. A Pew Research Center study found that Baby Boomers' favorite identifying mark was their work ethic, while only 5 percent of my generation reported the same. In contrast, 24 percent of Millennials chose "technology use," 11 percent

Millennials' Workplace Preferences

A survey asked 943 Millennial students from ten universities across the country to rate the following job characteristics on the level of importance they attach to each characteristic.

Rank	Characteristic	Average Score
1	Job Security	1.4
2	Boss that respects me	1.4
3	Boss that I respect	1.5
4	Clear guidance on what is expected	1.5
5	Ethical company	1.6
6	Above average pay and rewards	1.7
7	Good health insurance	1.7
8	Family friendly policies and benefits	1.9
9	Work that's fun	1.9
10	Collegial work environment	2.1
11	Frequent feedback on how I'm doing	2.1
12	Freedom to work how, when and where I choose	2.4
13	Plenty of time off	2.4

Key: 1=Very Important, 2=Important, 3=Little Importance, 4=Unimportant, 5=Very Unimportant

TAKEN FROM: Nancy Sutton Bell, J.A. Connell, Nathan E. McMinn, "How Will the Next Generation Change the Business World? A Report on a Survey," *Insights to a Changing World Journal*, no. 5, March 2011.

"music/pop culture," and 7 percent "liberal/tolerant" as their mark of distinction.

I can think of many things I'd like to be remembered for. "Technology use" isn't one of them.

A *New York Times* story from 2009 showed that many college graduates are turning down positions that don't meet a set of unrealistic expectations. One Syracuse University graduate rejected a $50,000-a-year job at a consulting firm "because he hadn't connected well with his potential bosses." Connection is for your spouse or cell phone, not your supervisor in a more-than-decent-paying job.

In a comprehensive review of Millennials' jobs plight, the *Atlantic* concluded that my generation has high income expectations mixed with low work expectations:

> Jean Twenge, an associate professor of psychology at San Diego State University, has carefully compared the attitudes of today's young adults to those of previous generations when they were the same age. Using national survey data, she's found that to an unprecedented degree, people who graduated from high school in the 2000s dislike the idea of work for work's sake, and expect jobs and career to be tailored to their interests and lifestyle. Yet they also have much higher material expectations than previous generations, and believe financial success is extremely important.

The 20s

The 20s are a great time to "cast about" in search of a life calling, but the exploration needs to end at some point. In contemporary culture, that decade has become a second adolescence, a notion reinforced by Obamacare's extension of parents' health-insurance benefits to 26-year-olds. Adults find a job and stick with it, even on bad days when it doesn't help them self-actualize.

Prior to the Sexual Revolution, young men and women had excellent reasons to keep a job and work hard: family responsibilities. In the 1940s, men on average married at age 24 and women at 22. Now, it stands at age 28 for men and 26 for women. Increasingly, those who do get married delay childbearing.

Once seen as a benchmark that signified passage to adulthood, marriage meant leaving parents and assuming responsibility for another human being. It was, and still is, a stabilizing influence on society. But with Millennials' delay of marriage has come a delay of adulthood. If no job is waiting after they graduate college, or if it's a job they don't like, Millennials can always move back in with mom and dad.

"It's a safety net—or safety diaper—that allows kids to quickly opt out of a job they don't like," said reporter Morley Safer on *60 Minutes*.

Columnist Ruben Navarrette, writing on CNN.com, neatly summarized the tendency: "Many millennials have been known to hold out for the perfect job at the perfect company with the perfect salary and a clear path to the vice presidency, even if that means crashing with mom and dad well into their 20s."

So much for the independent American work ethic. More times than not, it isn't until we've amassed burdensome debt or frittered away our 20s playing video games and buying $5 lattes that we understand that real life doesn't work that way.

It's time we stopped blaming external forces for our economic woes. Every generation has faced its version of a "raw deal"—whether it was the Great Depression and World War II for the Greatest Generation, or the Vietnam War and stagflation for the Boomers.

What matters is whether we shrug off the victim mentality and get our hands dirty making a better life for our loved ones and ourselves.

> "Digital natives have a different set of habits, standards, expectations, and social norms that stem from being raised in a culture deeply immersed in technology."

The Millennial Generation Is Productive in the Workplace

Brynn Evans

While many studies of the Millennial generation's work practices have criticized this generation for their poor work habits and inability to adapt to corporate life, in the viewpoint that follows, Brynn Evans refutes this stance and argues that their ways of working actually make them productive contributors to their workplaces. Evans examines three main areas in which these young workers differ from their older counterparts—they work any and everywhere; their leisure time is often spent online; and they are constantly connected to a broad social network through digital technology. These three main traits, Evans contends, provide the digital native with a unique ability to produce quality work in a world that is increasingly defined by digital technologies and connectivity, and those who know how to best utilize these advances will offer a distinct business advantage to their company. After working as a neuro-

psychologist for six years, Evans became a consultant focusing on human interaction with technology.

As you read, consider the following questions:
1. What is one of the main characteristics of the anywhere-everywhere work style as defined by Anne Zelenka and cited by Evans?
2. As cited by the author, what are the benefits of digital breaks found by Brent Coker?
3. What are the three distinct ways in which digital natives bring value to both themselves and their companies through online socializing as stated by Evans?

W hat exactly is a work practice? It's not a matter of what work gets done but rather how it gets done. It's the doing of the work; it's the process of producing; it's a frame of mind for dealing with the mundane as well as the urgent. Included in this frame of mind are habits, standards, expectations, and social norms. For example, a familiar standard is the one-hour lunch break. Additionally, there are certain workplace expectations, which may vary within enterprises (e.g., how quickly to respond to a coworker's email). Finally, basic social norms apply regardless of company culture (e.g., it's rude to be on Facebook during a client meeting).

However, digital natives have a different set of habits, standards, expectations, and social norms that stem from being raised in a culture deeply immersed in technology. While their differences may not always clash with non-natives, their work practice is unique and demands patience and compromise from non-natives to understand it and make the most of it. . . .

The Habits and Practices of a Digital Native

The following account depicts a young woman, Robin, whose childhood was filled with digital technologies, which were used for both work and play. Today, her behaviors reflect the attributes of a digital native, quite distinct from the attributes of workers from previous generations. As you read the following story, consider how Robin's upbringing might affect her current work practices:

> Robin is a 25-year-old technical project manager at Intuit. Growing up in a large family, she needed to jockey for attention with her three younger brothers. She took to video games as a way to compete with them, spending hours on gaming consoles and on the family computer late into the night. She was a natural with computers and even won a programming contest in high school. However, her intellectual passions were history and English.
>
> Her parents sent her to college with a personal laptop. It became her life. She used it for taking notes during class, researching material for writing assignments, and doing homework. It was with her in the dorm, on the front steps of the cafeteria, in the noisy student center, and in off-campus cafes. She never hesitated to call upon the trustworthy machine in the middle of a conversation (even once with the dean of her university) if she thought that Google or Wikipedia could resolve some pressing issue or embellish an important point.
>
> Her laptop was also her social lifeline. She kept Facebook a click away in an ever-present tab in her web browser. She'd check it during class and when stress caused her to wake up in the middle of the night. Now, only a few years out of college, Robin has more than 1,500 friends on Facebook, from high school, college, and various extracurricular activities. She hasn't spoken directly with many of them in years, but instead maintains a semi-complete awareness of their whereabouts and activities through continuous partial attention to their streams. It's a convenient, lightweight way to stay in touch.

Today, Robin is always connected, always online. It's a fast-paced lifestyle—no longer about gaming and programming but still deeply connected to technology. It's second nature to her. She doesn't know another life.

Unfortunately, her managers at Intuit aren't aware of these past experiences and are often confused by her work practice. She's not at her desk when they walk by at 9 AM on their way to get coffee. She always grabs her iPhone when she steps away from her desk. And she often sends emails to the team very late at night, though she does consistently produce good work on time. In recent months, her managers have noticed some exciting new technical ideas coming from her—not something they expected from a history major. Thus, they have resolved to put up with her "idiosyncrasies," even if they don't really "get" her.

What appear to Robin's managers as idiosyncrasies are actually the habits and practices of a digital native. This is her work practice, and it's something that she shares with other digital natives across the industry: Her work comes with her anywhere (and everywhere) she goes, and social activities play a central role in her life. This shouldn't come as too much of a surprise if you think about her day-to-day experiences in college: Robin worked wherever her laptop was (and her laptop was always with her), and she was always connected to her friends. . . .

Work Occurs Anywhere and Everywhere

The nature of "work" has changed a lot over the course of the past few centuries. This is most striking if we think about how our ancestors spent their waking hours just trying to meet their basic needs: finding food, making clothing, securing shelter. Significantly, much of today's work force performs information-based tasks, or knowledge work. Uday Apte and Hiranya Nath noted in their article, "Size, Structure and Growth of the U.S. Information Economy", that this type of work accounts for almost 70 percent of the U.S. labor force.

What's more, many types of knowledge work can now be done from anywhere and everywhere—across devices and across locations. Robin, for example, checks email on her iPhone first thing every morning. She uses this time to take care of urgent requests, provide her team and managers with status updates, and prepare herself for what's to come during the rest of the day. By starting her workday at home, she gets a head start on her projects, though she inevitably arrives "late" to the office.

Perhaps digital natives embrace this anywhere-everywhere mentality because they treat technology as a trusted partner in life rather than as an irritating mother-in-law. And yet, it's largely simple communication and networking technologies that make possible a distributed workplace. Laptops and netbooks, mobile phones, instant messenger (IM), Skype, virtual private network (VPN), Gmail, and cloud computing resources like Google Docs all support this networked lifestyle.

One of the characteristics of this work style is what Anne Zelenka from the blog *Web Worker Daily* calls "bursty work." Instead of working in four-hour continuous blocks, digital natives work in smaller chunks. Dawn Foster writes [on the tech news site GigaOM] that she intentionally splits her day into chunks so that she "can be productive for longer periods of time". Although this sounds counterintuitive, there is a rationale and structure behind her segmented work blocks.

Since meetings greatly disrupt her day, Foster has learned to set aside Mondays for meetings so that the rest of the week goes uninterrupted. When this isn't possible, she makes sure to leave a few solid hours in the morning before her first meeting, in order to complete her important client work first. She further batches her client work into smaller chunks, saving a number of client-related tasks for a continuous block of time, reporting that this "helps to avoid getting projects confused by jumping too quickly between clients.". . . .

It's important to note that bursty work is not the same as multitasking. Digital natives who break their work into smaller segments are not performing multiple tasks simultaneously. They're doing more focused work for smaller periods of time. I expect that we've all experienced this at some point, where one hour of dedicated work can be more productive than a workday full of interruptions. . . .

Digital Leisure Time Increases Productivity

Despite how it may sound, having a bursty work practice with an anywhere-everywhere mindset does not mean that digital natives are constantly working. Leisure time is taken in bursts as well. Digital natives log more hours at their computer (in total) but switch between work and leisure tasks in one sitting. . . .

Digital natives see technology as a tool that enables them to work or play, which results in their leisure time activities taking place via digital technologies. You're more likely to see them texting, IMing, Facebooking, or browsing the web at their computers in the middle of the workday than see them step out for coffee or take a walk around the block.

There are benefits to taking digital breaks. Dr. Brent Coker from the University of Melbourne observes that "people who surf the internet for fun at work—within a reasonable limit of less than 20 percent of their total time in the office—are more productive by about 9 percent than those who don't". Of course, leisure activities must take place in moderation, but they can lead to increased productivity because short breaks help us "zone out" for a while, so that we can return to our tasks with greater concentration afterward. Another benefit to digital breaks is that if your concentration returns or inspiration strikes in the midst of leisure time, you're already at the keyboard ready to capture your insights.

In sum, distributed networking technologies are creating an anywhere-everywhere work practice, leading to bursty work and digital leisure time. Digital natives take advantage of these opportunities to get a head start on their workday, to segment their time into meaningful chunks, and to gain perspective and reset their concentration after time away from a task.

The Emergence of "Social Permeance"

Having continuous connectivity with digital devices has both advantages and disadvantages. Receiving a phone call at 5 AM from someone in a different time zone is terribly inopportune. However, texting someone when you're running late for an appointment is wonderfully convenient.

What's really happening here is that these digital devices are creating a type of "social permeance"—an expression that conveys how social activities are beginning to permeate our everyday lives. Daily affairs as mundane as grocery shopping are steeped in social interactions, as the digitally equipped text their friends, tweet about what's happening, and broadcast the GPS coordinates of their locations. And their friends communicate back within minutes, if not seconds. Most of us feel that this trend makes it increasingly hard to separate out the professional from the personal. Digital natives don't think in these terms; instead, they find distinct advantages to this social culture.

Some of the same enablers of the anywhere-everywhere work mentality—advanced networking and mobile technologies—also support the social permeance trend. On social networking sites, people forge and strengthen connections with family and friends as well as acquaintances they've only met once. Texting, IMing, and video chatting with Skype are other popular ways for staying in touch throughout the day. A level of social continuity is maintained; it's this ongoing connection that provides unique benefits. . . .

Those digital breaks mentioned earlier are part of what makes continuous partial attention possible today. This is a very common habit and expectation of digital natives, and they don't consider it to be socially superficial or fake. Instead, it creates just enough of a connection that people begin to feel a sense of ambient intimacy. Clive Thompson of the *New York Times* writes about the significance of this in his article, "Brave New World of Digital Intimacy": Each little update—each individual bit of social information—is insignificant on its own, even supremely mundane. But taken together, over time, the little snippets coalesce into a surprisingly sophisticated portrait of your friends' and family members' lives, like thousands of dots making a pointillist painting. This was never before possible, because in the real world, no friend would bother to call you up and detail the sandwiches she was eating. The ambient information becomes like "a type of E.S.P."

Many non-natives would question the value in maintaining semi-complete accounts of the thousands of friends you've ever met. However, it is important to understand that, for the native, it's not just about the numbers—friends aren't like collectible trading cards. It's all about diversity—friends are more like the olive in a martini, infusing your environment with their distinctly flavored perspectives. Having a wide, diverse set of active ties is where the critical advantage lies.

The Workplace Benefits of Online Socializing

Digital natives, who attend social events and hang out with friends online are doing more than just socializing. They are establishing a remarkably diverse set of social peers, which brings value to them—and indirectly to their companies and managers—in at least three distinct ways.

First, it is the network of social ties from different industries, backgrounds, interests, and life stages that confers the nonredundant information advantage. Having a large network of professional contacts is not the same, since professionals within a single industry tend to flock together. In contrast, our first protagonist, Robin, keeps up with friends from high school, college, and beyond nearly every day. Even 15 years and a thousand new colleagues from now, her world will be composed largely of social ties.

Second, it's the act of socializing that helps spread ideas. Anyone can collect a thousand trading cards, but good things only come by actually playing those cards. Knowledge only gets transferred by keeping relationships active and having conversations. At that point, social ties represent both people resources and information resources. For example, Nathan-the-consultant had absorbed enough information from my BarCamp session to draft a lifetracking proposal for his client. Yet, I was also a direct "people" resource in his network, as he turned to me to get additional information.

Third, social interactions may actually improve our cognition. Dr. Oscar Ybarra and colleagues report as much in their article, "Mental Exercising Through Simple Socializing: Social Interaction Promotes General Cognitive Functioning". Their study was simple: 1) Subjects were divided into three groups; (2) each group performed a different, initial exercise; and 3) everyone was then given the same set of standard cognitive tests. The first group initially did a passive social exercise: Subjects sat silently watching an episode of *Seinfeld* (seated next to another subject). The second group did an active social exercise: Two subjects had a conversation together about privacy protection. The third group did an intellectual exercise: Subjects had to solve a crossword puzzle, perform mental rotations, and answer questions about a written passage.

Surprisingly, the researchers found that subjects who began with the active social exercise did just as well on the later cognitive tests as subjects who started with reading comprehension and crossword puzzles. Even more surprising was that merely observing passive social interactions did not improve cognitive performance. These findings suggest that interacting with friends may help us in more ways than one. Their knowledge is infectious and socializing may actually prime parts of our brains to help us with intellectual tasks.

In sum, social permeance is creating a culture of social continuity, in which digital natives maintain large, active networks with a diverse set of social peers. As a result, daily interactions create a sense of ambient intimacy and condition the mind, and represent people and information resources that can prove valuable in the future.

Utilizing Digital Technologies Drives Positive Change

So, how are digital natives transforming the way business is done? It's not just their hip iPhones and contemporary slang ("Facebook me!") that marks this as a new era. Their work practice is fundamentally changing as they live and breathe this culture of distributed networking and social technologies. It may never be a practice that managers and previous generations wish to embrace personally—and that's fine. They will, however, need to recognize and understand this emerging work practice if they wish to maximize the digital native work force.

The goal is to describe this emerging work style and highlight the role it plays in digital natives' success. An anywhere-everywhere mindset means that work is done in chunks, intermixed with leisure time. Leisure activities are often social: staying in touch with old friends and new acquaintances, and sharing intimate tidbits and interesting news stories. These social interactions help to spread ideas and improve problem-solving ability. The end result is that the digital technologies enabling this shift in work practice may actually be imparting a critical cognitive advantage to . . . employees and simultaneously driving innovation and creativity in . . . enterprise.

> "Generation Y grew up in the
> entrepreneurial shadow cast by Bill
> Gates and Steve Jobs and has been,
> in turn, inspired to start their own
> businesses."

The Millennial Generation Is Entrepreneurial

Rick Jensen

Instead of focusing on the Millennial generation's fitness for the workplace, in the viewpoint that follows, Rick Jensen makes the case that the youth of America will be defined by their entrepreneurial inclinations. Jensen contends that this generation, defined by its tech-savvy, connectedness, and independence, will be the leaders of new, small business start-ups and may in fact be the most entrepreneurial generation in the nation's history. This generation's skill and freedom to choose their own path, coupled with increasing support from educational institutions, have created the perfect foundation for these individuals to change the current state of business in America, according to the author. Jensen serves as the senior vice president and chief sales and marketing officer for the small business marketing and communication consulting company Constant Contact.

Rick Jensen, "Generation Y Digital Natives May Be Most Entrepreneurial Ever," *Washington Examiner*, August 24, 2008. WashingtonExaminer.com. Copyright © 2008 by Washington Examiner. All rights reserved. Reproduced by permission.

As you read, consider the following questions:

1. As stated by Jensen, why is "effortless multitasking" essential for entrepreneurs?
2. What does the author identify as the business world benefit of Generation Y's networking and communication style?
3. What role does education play in creating a generation of entrepreneurs, according to Jensen?

Get a job!" is not something most Gen Y-ers have heard. Instead of becoming job seekers, many members of this industrious group are becoming job creators, laying the groundwork to parlay their hobbies into careers.

By 2017, the stereotypical white, middle-aged men who traditionally started small businesses will be outnumbered by a newly emerging work force: Generation Y-ers—those born after 1982—women, immigrants and "un-retiring" baby boomers opting for entrepreneurship as a second career.

Some researchers predict that Generation Y will make the largest impact in the entrepreneurial world. In fact, the "Future of Small Business Report" says Gen Y may be the most entrepreneurial generation ever.

Raised to Be Entrepreneurs

Generation Y grew up in the entrepreneurial shadow cast by Bill Gates and Steve Jobs and has been, in turn, inspired to start their own businesses. This entrepreneurial interest, coupled with the innovations made possible by technology, gives this generation an unprecedented opportunity to shape the world of small business.

Three characteristics make Gen Y markedly different than its predecessors.

Tech-savvy. Gen Y is the first generation to grow up with digital technologies rather than having to adapt to them. From video games to digital music and the Internet, this generation knows no bounds with technology. They were born into a culture of multitasking—listening to an iPod, surfing the Net and text-messaging at the same time.

Effortless multitasking often is an essential survival skill for entrepreneurs; they must wear numerous hats to move a company forward. Familiarity with technology makes multitasking second nature.

Juggling multiple and diverse projects, such as balancing a company's books, running an advertising campaign and creating a Web site all in the same day, are not far-fetched for this innovative group.

Networked. Gen Y is the most networked group in history. The Internet has replaced the campus, coffee shop or shopping mall as the social gathering place, spawning the creation and nurturing of hundreds of relationships around the world. New media, such as e-mail, blogs, alumni Web sites and social networks, make it relatively easy to connect with anyone from their past.

Quite simply, the Gen Y-ers' network is exponentially larger than that of their parents and predecessors. Socially, Gen Y-ers depend on relationships with a select but changeable group of peers.

Communications today are often group-oriented: one-to-many rather than one-to-one. Instead of contacting individuals sequentially, Gen Y-ers reach out to many with the same message.

Though this may seem impersonal, it allows these 20-somethings to keep tabs on a much larger group with less effort. This lifestyle relies on peers to share news, ideas and opportunities.

In the business world, this dialogue can prove invaluable to entrepreneurs, allowing them to approach their entire network with business ideas, partnership or consumer ideas. Finding a base population to grow their business is one of the big challenges facing entrepreneurs. But Gen Y's networked lifestyle holds the ingredients for a ready-made group of business partners, test markets and customers.

Freedom and Independence Breed Entrepreneurial Spirit

Independent. Lastly, Gen Y-ers seek independence. They are leery of working in the corporate world and see traditional "big company" jobs as both constraining and risky. They want to chart their own destiny, which works out well as the business world becomes more complex.

As businesses become more sophisticated and need more specialized skills, Gen Y can fill that need by focusing solely on their own niche or skill and build companies based on that expertise.

For example, Mark Zuckerberg created Facebook in 2004 as a way to network his Harvard classmates. Today [August 2008], the site boasts some 80 million users worldwide with revenue estimated at $150 million.

Gen Y-ers enjoy freedoms few other generations have experienced, mainly the independence to follow whatever path they choose.

They have an enormous network and specialized skills; why would they work for anyone but themselves?

Confident and innovative, many Gen Y-ers are natural-born risk-takers, unafraid to chase dreams in their personal or professional lives.

They are socially networked, tech-savvy multitaskers who believe that all outcomes are possible.

And this trend toward entrepreneurial job creators will continue as colleges offer students more courses with specialized degrees. There are 27 million small businesses in the United States today, a number that is expected to continue growing over the next 10 years.

Given the importance of small business to the nation's economy, it's important that the emerging Gen Y entrepreneurs receive the educational and career guidance they need to support their dreams.

Is Generation Y the new Greatest Generation? Time will tell. But one thing is certain: Gen Y is changing the business world in a way that no other has.

Periodical Bibliography

The following articles have been selected to supplement the diverse views presented in this chapter.

Erica Alini	"Generation Spend," *Maclean's*, November 15, 2010.
ASHRAE Journal	"Gen Y Wants Different Type of Workplace," July 2010.
Carey Benedict	"A Snapshot of a Generation May Come Out Blurry," *New York Times*, August 3, 2010.
Michael Crowley and Hector Florin	"The New Generation Gap," *Time*, November 14, 2011.
Economist	"The Net Generation, Unplugged," March 6, 2010.
Ben Little	"The Millennial Generation and Politics," *Soundings*, Summer 2009.
Kimberly Palmer	"Talking to Gen Y about the New Culture of Thrift," *US News & World Report*, March 2010.
Larry Rosen	"Understanding the iGeneration—Before the Next Mini-Generation Arrives," *Nieman Reports*, Summer 2010.
Mashaun D. Simon and Brittany Hutson	"Swing Vote?," *Black Enterprise*, October 2008.
USA Today Magazine	"Another Fine Mess for Generation Y," December 2008.
Jeffrey Zaslow	"The Greatest Generation (of Networkers)," *Wall Street Journal*, November 4, 2009.

CHAPTER 2

How Motivated and Well Educated Is the Millennial Generation?

Chapter Preface

Anna Ivey, a former dean of admissions at the University of Chicago Law School, runs a consulting firm to help young people get into top universities. On her consulting firm's website, Ivey claims she knows the character of the new generation—the Millennials, even offering advice to employers who have problems motivating young people in the workplace. According to Ivey's counsel, Millennials need to function in groups and "hate making decisions by themselves." She insists their writing skills are "atrocious," and they need help communicating face-to-face with clients or business partners. Ivey also maintains that Millennials need to be praised constantly for good work and even flattered because they supposedly think "very highly of themselves." She acknowledges that Generation Y workers are capable and diligent, but she warns that they also consider themselves "free agents," willing to jump ship if a job doesn't live up to their high expectations.

Ivey's suggestions are not unusual or even unprecedented. Numerous websites offer similar advice to business managers who will undoubtedly face the hundred million Millennial-generation employees in the United States alone. Career columnist Penelope Trunk begins a June 9, 2009, *Bloomberg Businessweek* article by stating, "Young people change jobs every 18 months. And when they get a job, they start job hunting three days after their start date." Like Ivey, Trunk insists that Generation Y workers are competent and accomplished but only if they are guided—even "micromanaged"—and rewarded. Otherwise, she fears they get bored and will seek interests elsewhere.

Most analysts like Ivey and Trunk believe the motivational needs of the Millennial generation derive from how they were reared and educated. Their desire to work in teams supposedly comes from being schooled in the benefits of collective problem solving, and their parents are to blame for their expectation of praise and guidance for each task. Some analysts believe Millennials' have a need for variety in the workplace because their home lives have been filled with soccer practice, science fairs, karate classes, and every other diversion their parents could afford. All these influences have purportedly created workers who need special attention in order to be productive.

However, some see these generational traits as a boon to the workplace environment. In *Millennials in the Workplace*, authors Neil Howe and Reena Nadler describe how many businesses are courting Millennials and adopting office spaces to their particular quirks. In an interview with American Public Media's *Marketplace*, Nadler said, "Millennials have a lot to offer America's workplaces." She points out that the desire to work in groups is tantamount to being a team player, a workplace characteristic that companies have always prized. Howe and Nadler assert that Millennials are usually well-educated and go into jobs with confidence that they will perform well, an expectation that stems from all those afterschool activities in which they were encouraged to do their best.

In the following chapter, authors debate the motivational drives of the Millennial Generation and further explore whether today's young adults are educated enough to tackle the responsibilities of work and civic engagement.

> *"The particulars vary, but young
> people from all walks of life are feeling
> the strain [of the globally competitive
> world]."*

The Millennial Generation
Is Highly Motivated and
Overwhelmed with Work

Sharon Jayson

*In the following viewpoint, Sharon Jayson makes the case that the
Millennial generation is under much higher levels of stress, particularly with regard to their education and success, than previous generations. In particular, Jayson cites numerous experts who have found
that this generation has experienced increasing pressure to achieve
academically not only in the face of expanding global competition
and parental expectations, but in response to personal expectations.
This pressure has created a culture of overachievers, according to an
author referenced by Jayson. While the experts note a stronger tendency of this experience in more affluent areas, they maintain that
socio-economic considerations are only one factor contributing to
the problem and have observed individuals across the spectrum ex-
periencing equal levels of stress associated with the push to succeed.
Jayson is the behaviors and relationships reporter for* USA Today.

As you read, consider the following questions:

1. According to Suniya Luthar as cited by Jayson, what combination of factors has led to an "especially anxiety-prone generation"?
2. How do the stress levels of today's youth compare with that of previous generations, according to the author?
3. How should parents and schools deal with youths' increasing level of stress according to the experts cited by Jayson?

Seventeen-year-old Alex Capp of Grosse Pointe, Mich., hopes his senior year of high school will be less stressful than his junior year.

"It was a pretty overwhelming workload," he says.

Besides taking two Advanced Placement classes, honors chemistry, math and electives, he served on the student council organizing community service projects, took a cultural diversity class at a community college for college credit, participated in his school's alcohol awareness group, did volunteer work, took tennis lessons and held down a part-time job.

He hasn't had too much rest this summer, either; it was largely spent building up his credentials for college. He took a summer school class, volunteered, worked at his dad's office and completed parts of the Common Application for the 10 or so colleges he's applying to.

"I wanted an extra English class on my transcript," he says.

A Generation Overwhelmed

For Capp's generation, "overwhelming" is par for the course. And those who study teens and people in their early 20s say young people are plenty stressed out.

They're coming of age in a globally competitive world where the path to the middle class is no longer a high school diploma. More students go to college; it's also costly and more selective, and they know it can change their lives. The particulars vary, but young people from all walks of life are feeling the strain.

"What contemporary American culture advertises is achievement and accomplishment as the route to ultimate happiness," says Suniya Luthar, a professor of psychology and education at Columbia University in New York.

She has spent much of the past decade studying affluent young people and comparing them with other socioeconomic groups. Luthar and others say a host of factors have resulted in an especially anxiety-prone generation, dealing with not just a faster-paced, technology-dominated society but also with their own lofty aspirations and their parents' expectations.

Some say these kids are too fragile as the result of overly involved parents who have rescued their children all too often, directing their lives and stunting their ability to rebound from difficulty.

But Luthar disagrees.

"Something else is going on that is really quite powerful," she says. "Much has to do with adolescents' internalized feelings of perfectionism and how much they want to accomplish. It is wrong to simply blame the parents."

The Plague of Pressure

Although experts say parents' anxiety has increased, social historian William Strauss, co-author of several books about the so-called millennial generation, says kids today also are more eager to please their parents than boomers were.

"They're under enormous pressure not just to succeed, but to be outstanding in everything they do," says Madeline Levine, a psychologist from Marin County, Calif., who has counseled young people for 25 years in private practice.

Data show that more young people are diagnosed with mental health problems, but Luanne Southern of the National Mental Health Association says the increase could be attributable to greater public awareness about mental health.

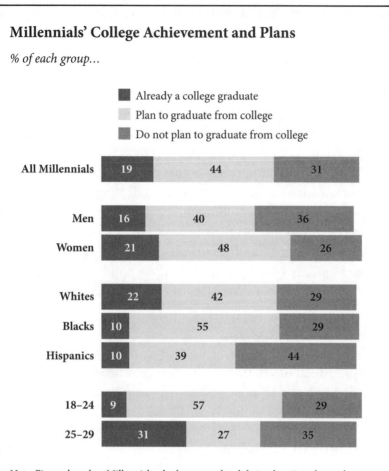

Millennials' College Achievement and Plans

% of each group...

■ Already a college graduate
□ Plan to graduate from college
■ Do not plan to graduate from college

	Already a college graduate	Plan to graduate from college	Do not plan to graduate from college
All Millennials	19	44	31
Men	16	40	36
Women	21	48	26
Whites	22	42	29
Blacks	10	55	29
Hispanics	10	39	44
18–24	9	57	29
25–29	31	27	35

Note: Figures based on Millennials who have completed their education, those who are still in school and those who are out of school but plan to return.

TAKEN FROM: Pew Research Center, "Millennials: A Portrait of Generation Next," February 2010.

A study by psychologists at Kansas State University published three years ago found that the number of college-age students treated for depression doubled from 1989 to 2001. And the University of Michigan Depression Center estimates that as many as 15% of college students are depressed.

Whether they're actually more anxiety-ridden than their parents or grandparents at similar ages isn't clear; such data have been collected only since the late 1950s, says Mike Bradley, an adolescent psychologist in Philadelphia and author of *The Heart & Soul of the Next Generation*, to be published next month.

But "since they've been collecting reliable data, kids are clearly more stressed and anxious than they've ever been," he says.

Bradley notes that not all stress is bad; it's the level of stress combined with biological and environmental factors that determines whether it will catapult into a mental disorder. He says use of prescription drugs to enhance academic performance and cope with the stress is "widespread" at colleges. A survey in 2005 by the Partnership for a Drug-Free America found that 19% of teens reported having taken prescription drugs, including stimulants such as Ritalin or Adderall. Those drugs, in addition to Provigil, are among the ones students use to boost concentration and memory during tests.

Psychologist Sherry Benton, assistant director of the counseling service at Kansas State University, studies student mental health. The higher a student's grade point average, the more likely he or she is to seek help, Benton says. More than half of the center's clients have GPAs of 3.2 or better.

"They do pretty well and think 'I can take on a little more,'" she says. "They're afraid they'll lose their edge. They think they can get by with a little less sleep. Pretty soon they're skipping meals. They don't exercise. They have no recovery time. It's all stress. Run, run, run."

The Overachiever Culture

Emily McConnell knows what can happen when the pressure is too great.

"I had a nervous breakdown in my senior year," says McConnell, 21, of Salt Lake City.

That emotional crisis caused her to drop out of her high school's International Baccalaureate program, an advanced curriculum that results in a prestigious IB diploma.

"I only did seven APs, which is not much for my school," she says. "Most people did the full IB diploma and seven AP classes."

She says she was diagnosed with clinical depression and has responded well to antidepressants.

She will graduate in May with a biology degree from St. Olaf College in Northfield, Minn. Then she plans to go to medical school.

She spent a month this summer with her grandmother in Louisville, cooking, doing needlework and writing poetry and fiction to "de-stress." She also spent two weeks earning her basic certification as an emergency medical technician.

"I'm a high achiever—not because I thrive on pressure but because I have lofty goals for myself," McConnell says.

Pressure in high school is all too common, she says.

"There's the sense that if you don't have a longer list of activities than everybody else, colleges are going to bump you down, and to be successful, you have to drive yourself crazy."

No, you don't, says Alexandra Robbins, author of the new book *The Overachievers: The Secret Lives of Driven Kids*. Robbins, 30, traveled the country and found a universal attitude of what she calls an "overachiever culture."

"You will find more of the overachiever culture in privileged areas because they're so driven toward getting into a prestigious school, but it transcends class lines," Robbins says.

"The goals can be different, but the poor students I met in eastern New Mexico were just as stressed and overwhelmed as the students in Bethesda, Md."

Emotional Support Is Necessary

Adora Mora, 18, comes from a family of high achievers in Columbus, Ohio. Her parents, an accountant and a pharmacist, emigrated from Nigeria. Their eight children are 11 to 24. The oldest graduated from medical school and has begun a medical residency. Another works at Tufts University, her alma mater, and another graduated from the Wharton School at the University of Pennsylvania and starts work this fall in New York. One is studying music composition at the Berklee College of Music in Boston; another attends Ohio State. All, including Adora, earned scholarships.

Adora, who is headed to Harvard as a freshman this fall, was salutatorian of her parochial high school. She also held her share of school leadership posts, did community service and worked, helping kids in an after-school program.

Much of her own drive has been spurred by peer pressure. "Once you do well, people always expect you to do well," she says.

Some experts, including Levine and Bradley, say particularly driven kids who don't know how to cope with stress may fall into risky behaviors or develop mental disorders. Levine's new book, *The Price of Privilege*, suggests the affluent, in particular, have high rates of depression, substance abuse, eating disorders and suicide.

Levine and Robbins say high schools, colleges and parents need to focus less on competition, performance and success and more on emotional support.

"The culture has come to view teenagers as small adults. They're not. They're large children," Bradley adds. (Recent research suggests the brain isn't fully developed until about age 25.) But Robbins says tendencies to overachieve in school carry over into the real world.

"They were left feeling if they couldn't be a success by age 25, then they were failures," she says.

Lost Youth

Capp is still working to improve his college prospects by boosting his standardized test scores. He has already taken the ACT "a couple of times," and "I think I'll take it again to see if my score will go up a little more." He also took the SAT and says he might take it again, too.

Such anxiety even shows up in market research, says Ian Pierpoint of Synovate, an international market research firm whose recent work has focused on ages 16 to 25.

"People don't seem to be enjoying their youth anymore," he says. "It's this 'I can't wait till I'm 30 and life will be sorted.' Being 22 just isn't much fun."

*"Young Americans today are no
more learned or skillful than their
predecessors, no more knowledgeable,
fluent, up-to-date, or inquisitive, except
in the materials of youth culture."*

The Millennial Generation
Is Not a Group of
Motivated Overachievers

Mark Bauerlein

*In contrast to reports that American youth are motivated over-
achievers, Mark Bauerlein argues in the viewpoint that follows
that the current generation of young Americans is actually declin-
ing in intelligence. This downward spiral, he contends, has resulted
from the continuously emerging and growing digital culture that
allows this generation to remain fully absorbed in youth culture
and themselves. Further, he emphasizes that they do not utilize
these digital technologies to enhance their knowledge, only their
connections with others in their social group; thus, he believes that
while the time is ripe for these individuals to capitalize on their
ever improving conduct—decreasing prejudice and risk behaviors
and increasing volunteer work for example—they are failing to*

Mark Bauerlein, *The Dumbest Generation*. New York: Penguin Group, 2008, pp. 1–10.
Copyright © 2008 by Penguin Group. All rights reserved. Reproduced by permission.

seize the opportunity to grow intellectually, civically, and cultur-
ally. Bauerlein is an English professor at Emory University.

As you read, consider the following questions:

1. According to the author, what did the *High School Survey of Student Engagement* and the *NAEP 2004 Trends in Academic Progress* reveal about the amount of time students spent doing homework?
2. Why is the tendency of older generations to berate the youth "a healthy process" according to the author?
3. What does the author believe to be the cost of American youth's "autonomy"?

When writer Alexandra Robbins returned to Walt Whitman High School in Bethesda, Maryland, ten years after graduating, she discovered an awful trend. The kids were miserable. She remembers her high school years as a grind of study and homework, but lots more, too, including leisure times that allowed for "well-roundedness." Not for Whitman students circa 2005. The teens in *The Overachievers*, Robbins's chronicle of a year spent among them, have only one thing on their minds, SUCCESS, and one thing in their hearts, ANXIETY. Trapped in a mad "culture of overachieverism," they run a frantic race to earn an A in every class, score 750 or higher on the SATs, take piano lessons, chalk up AP courses on their transcripts, stay in shape, please their parents, volunteer for outreach programs, and, most of all, win entrance to "HYP" (Harvard-Yale-Princeton). . . .

These kids have descended into a "competitive frenzy," Robbins mourns, and the high school that should open their minds and develop their characters has become a torture zone, a "hotbed for Machiavellian strategy." They bargain and bully and suck up for better grades. They pay tutors and coaches enormous sums to raise their scores a few points and help with the admissions process. Parents hover and query, and they schedule their children down to the minute. Grade inflation only makes it worse, an A- average now a stigma, not an accomplishment. They can't relax, they can't play. It's killing them, throwing sensitive and intelligent teenagers into pathologies of guilt and despair. The professional rat race of yore—men in gray flannel suits climbing the business ladder—has filtered down into the pre-college years, and Robbins's tormented subjects reveal the consequences.

The Organization Kids Must Achieve

The achievement chase displaces other life questions, and the kids can't seem to escape it. When David Brooks toured Princeton and interviewed students back in 2001, he heard of joyless days and nights with no room for newspapers or politics or dating, just "one skill-enhancing activity to the next." He calls them "Organization Kids" (after the old Organization Man figure of the fifties), students who "have to schedule appointment times for chatting." They've been programmed for success, and a preschool-to-college gauntlet of standardized tests, mounting homework, motivational messages, and extracurricular tasks has rewarded or punished them at every stage. The system tabulates learning incessantly and ranks students against one another, and the students soon divine its essence: only results matter. . . .

Just get the grades, they tell themselves, ace the test, study, study, study. Assignments become exercises to complete, like doing the dishes, not knowledge to acquire for the rest of their lives. The inner life fades; only the external credits count. After-school hours used to mean sports and comic books and hanging out. Now, they spell homework. As the president of the American Association of School Librarians told the *Washington Post*, "When kids are in school now, the stakes are so high, and they have so much homework that it's really hard to find time for pleasure reading". . . .

Parents, teachers, media, and the kids themselves witness the dangers, but the system presses forward. "We believe that reform in homework practices is central to a politics of family and personal liberation," Kralovec and Buell announce, but the momentum is too strong. The overachievement culture, results-obsessed parents, outcomes-based norms . . . they continue to brutalize kids and land concerned observers such as Robbins on the *Today* show. Testing goes on, homework piles up, and competition for spaces in the Ivies was stiffer in 2007 than ever before. A 2006 survey by Pew Research, for instance, found that more than half the adults in the United States (56 percent) think that parents place too little pressure on students, and only 15 percent stated "Too much."

Out-of-Class Preparation Is Lacking

Why?

Because something is wrong with this picture, and most people realize it. They sense what the critics do not, a fundamental error in the vignettes of hyperstudious and overworked kids that we've just seen: they don't tell the truth, not the whole truth about youth in America. For, notwithstanding the poignant tale of suburban D.C. seniors sweating over a calculus quiz, or the image of college students scheduling their friends as if they were CEOs in the middle of a workday, or the lurid complaints about homework, the actual habits of most teenagers and young adults in most schools and colleges in this country display a wholly contrasting problem, but one no less disturbing.

Consider a measure of homework time, this one not taken from a dozen kids on their uneven way to the top, but from 81,499 students in 110 schools in 26 states—the 2006 *High School Survey of Student Engagement*. When asked how many hours they spent each week "Reading/studying for class," almost all of them, fully 90 percent, came in at a ridiculously low five hours or less, 55 percent at one hour or less. Meanwhile, 31 percent admitted to watching television or playing video games at least six hours per week, 25 percent of them logging six hours minimum surfing and chatting online.

Or check a 2004 report by the University of Michigan Institute for Social Research entitled *Changing Times of American Youth: 1981–2003*, which surveyed more than 2,000 families with children age six to 17 in the home. In 2003, homework time for 15- to 17-year-olds hit only 24 minutes on weekend days, 50 minutes on weekdays. And weekday TV time? More than twice that: one hour, 55 minutes.

Or check a report by the U.S. Department of Education entitled *NAEP 2004 Trends in Academic Progress*. Among other things, the report gathered data on study and reading time for thousands of 17-year-olds in 2004. When asked how many hours they'd spent on homework the day before, the tallies were meager. Fully 26 percent said that they didn't have any homework to do, while 13 percent admitted that they didn't do any of the homework they were supposed to. A little more than one-quarter (28 percent) spent less than an hour, and another 22 percent devoted one to two hours, leaving only 11 percent to pass the two-hour mark.

Or the 2004–05 *State of Our Nation's Youth* report by the Horatio Alger Association, in which 60 percent of teenage students logged five hours of homework per week or less.

The better students don't improve with time, either. In the 2006 *National Survey of Student Engagement*, a college counterpart to the *High School Survey of Student Engagement*, seniors in college logged some astonishingly low commitments to "Preparing for class." Almost one out of five (18 percent) stood at one to five hours per week, and 26 percent at six to ten hours per week. College professors estimate that a successful semester requires about 25 hours of out-of-class study per week, but only 11 percent reached that mark. These young adults have graduated from high school, entered college, declared a major, and lasted seven semesters, but their in-class and out-of-class punch cards amount to fewer hours than a part-time job.

The Overachievement Culture
Is a Myth

And as for the claim that leisure time is disappearing, the Bureau of Labor Statistics issues an annual *American Time Use Survey* that asks up to 21,000 people to record their activities during the day. The categories include work and school and child care, and also leisure hours. For 2005, 15- to 24-year-olds enjoyed a full five and a half hours of free time per day, more than two hours of which they passed in front of the TV.

The findings of these and many other large surveys refute the frantic and partial renditions of youth habits and achievement that all too often make headlines and fill talk shows. Savvier observers guard against the "we're overworking the kids" alarm, people such as Jay Mathews, education reporter at the *Washington Post*, who called Robbins's book a "spreading delusion," and Tom Loveless of the Brookings Institution, whose 2003 report on homework said of the "homework is destroying childhood" argument, "Almost everything in this story is wrong." One correspondent's encounter with a dozen elite students who hunt success can be vivid and touching, but it doesn't jibe with mountains of data that tell contrary stories. The surveys, studies, tests, and testimonials reveal the opposite, that the vast majority of high school and college kids are far less accomplished and engaged, and the classroom pressures much less cumbersome, than popular versions put forth. These depressing accounts issue from government agencies with no ax to grind, from business leaders who just want competent workers, and from foundations that sympathize with the young. While they lack the human drama, they impart more reliable assessments, providing a better baseline for understanding the realities of the young American mentality and forcing us to stop upgrading the adolescent condition beyond its due.

The Downward Intellectual Trend

This . . . is an attempt to consolidate the best and broadest research into a different profile of the rising American mind. It doesn't cover behaviors and values, only the intellect of under-30-year-olds. Their political leanings don't matter, nor do their career ambitions. The manners, music, clothing, speech, sexuality, faith, diversity, depression, criminality, drug use, moral codes, and celebrities of the young spark many books, articles, research papers, and marketing strategies centered on Generation Y (or Generation DotNet, or the Millennials), but not this one. It sticks to one thing, the intellectual condition of young Americans, and describes it with empirical evidence, recording something hard to document but nonetheless insidious happening inside their heads. The information is scattered and underanalyzed, but once collected and compared, it charts a consistent and perilous momentum downward.

It sounds pessimistic. . . . Older people have complained forever about the derelictions of youth, and the "old fogy" tag puts them on the defensive. Perhaps, though, it is a healthy process in the life story of humanity for older generations to berate the younger, for young and old to relate in a vigorous competitive dialectic, with the energy and optimism of youth vying against the wisdom and realism of elders in a fruitful check of one another's worst tendencies. That's another issue, however. The conclusions here stem from a variety of completed and ongoing research projects, public and private organizations, and university professors and media centers, and they represent different cultural values and varying attitudes toward youth. It is remarkable, then, that they so often reach the same general conclusions. They disclose many trends and consequences in youth experience, but the intellectual one emerges again and again. It's an outcome not as easily noticed as a carload of teens inching down the boulevard rattling store windows with the boom-boom of a hip-hop beat, and the effect runs deeper than brand-name clothing and speech patterns. It touches the core of a young person's mind, the mental storehouse from which he draws when engaging the world. And what the sources reveal, one by one, is that a paradoxical and distressing situation is upon us.

Information but Not Knowledge Has Increased

The paradox may be put this way. We have entered the Information Age, traveled the Information Superhighway, spawned a Knowledge Economy, undergone the Digital Revolution, converted manual workers into knowledge workers, and promoted a Creative Class, and we anticipate a Conceptual Age to be. However overhyped those grand social metaphors, they signify a rising premium on knowledge and communications, and everyone from *Wired* magazine to Al Gore to Thomas Friedman to the Task Force on the Future of American Innovation echoes the change. When he announced the American Competitiveness Initiative in February 2006, President [George W.] Bush directly linked the fate of the U.S. economy "to generating knowledge and tools upon which new technologies are developed." In a *Washington Post* op-ed, Bill Gates asserted, "But if we are to remain competitive, we need a workforce that consists of the world's brightest minds. . . . First, we must demand strong schools so that young Americans enter the workforce with the math, science and problem-solving skills they need to succeed in the knowledge economy."

And yet, while teens and young adults have absorbed digital tools into their daily lives like no other age group, while they have grown up with more knowledge and information readily at hand, taken more classes, built their own Web sites, enjoyed more libraries, bookstores, and museums in their towns and cities . . . in sum, while the world has provided them extraordinary chances to gain knowledge and improve their reading/ writing skills, not to mention offering financial incentives to do so, young Americans today are no more learned or skillful than their predecessors, no more knowledgeable, fluent, up-to-date, or inquisitive, except in the materials of youth culture. They don't know any more history or civics, economics or science, literature or current events. They read less on their own, both books and newspapers, and you would have to canvass a lot of college English instructors and employers before you found one who said that they compose better paragraphs. In fact, their technology skills fall well short of the common claim, too, especially when they must apply them to research and workplace tasks.

The Opportunity to Advance Exists

The world delivers facts and events and art and ideas as never before, but the young American mind hasn't opened. Young Americans' vices have diminished, one must acknowledge, as teens and young adults harbor fewer stereotypes and social prejudices. Also, they regard their parents more highly than they did 25 years ago. They volunteer in strong numbers, and rates of risky behaviors are dropping. Overall conduct trends are moving upward, leading a hard-edged commentator such as Kay Hymowitz to announce in "It's Morning After in America" that "pragmatic Americans have seen the damage that their decades-long fling with the sexual revolution and the transvaluation of traditional values wrought. And now, without giving up the real gains, they are earnestly knitting up their unraveled culture. It is a moment of tremendous promise." At *TechCentralStation .com*, James Glassman agreed enough to proclaim, "Good News! The Kids Are Alright!" Youth watchers William Strauss and Neil Howe were confident enough to subtitle their book on young Americans *The Next Great Generation*.

And why shouldn't they? Teenagers and young adults mingle in a society of abundance, intellectual as well as material. American youth in the twenty-first century have benefited from a shower of money and goods, a bath of liberties and pleasing self-images, vibrant civic debates, political blogs, old books and masterpieces available online, traveling exhibitions, the History Channel, news feeds . . . and on and on. Never have opportunities for education, learning, political action, and cultural activity been greater. All the ingredients for making an informed and intelligent citizen are in place.

Youth Culture Consumes a Generation

But it hasn't happened. Yes, young Americans are energetic, ambitious, enterprising, and good, but their talents and interests and money thrust them not into books and ideas and history and civics, but into a whole other realm and other consciousness. A different social life and a different mental life have formed among them. Technology has bred it, but the result doesn't tally with the fulsome descriptions of digital empowerment, global awareness, and virtual communities. Instead of opening young American minds to the stores of civilization and science and politics, technology has contracted their horizon to themselves, to the social scene around them. Young people have never been so intensely mindful of and present to one another, so enabled in adolescent contact. Teen images and songs, hot gossip and games, and youth-to-youth communications no longer limited by time or space wrap them up in a generational cocoon reaching all the way into their bedrooms. The autonomy has a cost: the more they attend to themselves, the less they remember the past and envision a future. They have all the advantages of modernity and democracy, but when the gifts of life lead to social joys, not intellectual labor, the minds of the young plateau at age 18. This is happening all around us. The fonts of knowledge are everywhere, but the rising generation is camped in the desert, passing stories, pictures, tunes, and texts back and forth, living off the thrill of peer attention. Meanwhile, their intellects refuse the cultural and civic inheritance that has made us what we are up to now.

"Somehow, schools have decided that all the light that surrounds kids—that is, their electronic connections to the world—is somehow detrimental to their education."

Education for the Millennial Generation Should Reflect Its Digital Upbringing

Marc Prensky

In 2001 education writer Marc Prensky coined the terms digital natives and digital immigrants in the On the Horizon *article "Digital Natives, Digital Immigrants: A New Way to Look at Ourselves and Our Kids." He describes the differences between the generation of individuals born into a world of digital technologies and those who had to adapt to this new world. This digital generation, he argues in the following viewpoint, needs to be educated using new methods that coincide with their digital upbringing. He advocates for more digitally based learning with less focus on content and more focus on engagement. He urges educators to teach with modern technological tools to keep up with current trends and to prepare students to understand and make the most of the digital world they*

Marc Prensky, "Turning on the Lights," *Educational Leadership*, vol. 65, no. 6, March 2008, pp. 40–45. Copyright © 2008 by Association for Supervision and Curriculum Development (ASCD). All rights reserved. Reproduced by permission.

already inhabit. If educators willingly listen to their technologically savvy students about how to utilize digital technologies in schools, Prensky believes meaningful education for the generation of digital natives can occur.

As you read, consider the following questions:

1. What are the elements of the "darkness of the old-fashioned classroom" with which Prensky claims most modern students are forced to engage?
2. What are three examples of the "after school" learning that Prensky describes?
3. How does Prensky advise educators to find out how today's students want to be taught?

For most of history, kids grew up in the dark intellectually. Right up until the mid-20th century, when television became widespread, the world outside their own neighborhoods was largely unknown to them. Few traveled. Some heard tales of adventure, war, or derring-do. Many parents told stories of just how dangerous "out there" really was. Few young people read widely. In terms of knowing the world you lived in, as a kid you were pretty much left in the dark.

Until you got to school.

That was the beginning of your enlightenment—the day your window opened on the outside world. As you advanced in the grades, the window opened wider, and more and more light shone in. From your teachers, you learned wonderful things you knew to be true—because they told you so. They taught you to read and, as a result, more of the world became available to you. The images you came across in books and the artifacts you discovered in museums broadened your knowledge.

Over time, your teachers taught you how to conduct experiments, test ideas, and separate fact from fiction. They showed you systems and frameworks that would help you understand history, geography, mathematics, science, and your own and other cultures. You were exposed to civilization's greatest accomplishments and learned about famous men and women. You learned to think logically, structure your ideas and thoughts, and write them down for others to read and critique.

Not every kid found school interesting, of course, and some left earlier than others. But for a great many students, school was truly empowering. It exposed kids for the first time to a wide variety of useful things they knew nothing about, in ways that the students were unable to do on their own.

In fact, one of the key purposes of school was to lead as many kids as possible out of the intellectual darkness into the intellectual light. That is what made being an educator a truly noble calling: We were the people who showed the kids the light.

Technology Spreads Education

There's one big problem with this noble thought today: Today's kids grow up in the light. They're deeply immersed in it long before educators ever see them.

Kids today are connected to the entire world around the clock, in real time, through their media and their myriad personal devices, both electronic (such as TV) and digital (such as the Internet and cell phones). In the 21st century, young people certainly don't grow up with perfect understanding of the world—after all, they *are* still kids. But can we still characterize their intellectual state as one of ignorance and darkness? Hardly.

Thanks to technology, kids in developed countries grow up knowing about, or being able to find out about, pretty much anything from the past or present that interests them. Google, Wikipedia, and millions of reference sites stand at their beck and call.

Many 21st-century kids grow up literally *surrounded* by light, from the first flash of the camera at the moment of birth. They progress to seeing the world through the glow of the TV tube, the sheen of the silver screen, the interactive animations of the computer screen, the LCD on their cell phone, and the screens on their Game Boy Advance consoles, Nintendo DS Lites, and PlayStation Portable Systems. They teach one another to actively participate as often as possible in the world—locally and around the globe—through instant messaging, e-mails, and increasingly free telephone calls, as well as online connections, discussions, and creative social and communal activities that range from making and sharing music, to helping to slow global warming, to helping to stop genocide in Darfur.

Long before they ever get to school, kids have seen a tremendous amount of the world. They've watched wars in far-off countries and explorations of distant planets. They've seen wild animals up close. They've simulated racing, flying, and running businesses. Many have taught themselves to read through the electronic games they play.

The world is no longer a dark, unknown place for today's school kids. Kids are not intellectually empty. Even though some of what they know may be incomplete, biased, or wrong, they arrive at school full of knowledge, thoughts, ideas, and opinions about their world and their universe.

Schools Are Behind the Times

Given this new state of affairs, one might suppose that educators would acknowledge that today's kids grow up differently and that kids are enlightened by all their various connections to the world. Educators would figure out ways to use, build on, and strengthen students' reservoirs of knowledge. They would assume that kids will use their connections to the light to find information quickly, structure it in new ways, and communicate with peers around the world in a powerful, 21st-century learning process. Teachers would no longer be the providers of information but instead would be the explainers, the context providers, the meaning makers, and the evaluators of information that kids find on their own. Teaching would still be a noble calling, perhaps even more so than before.

But we've chosen something else. Somehow, schools have decided that all the light that surrounds kids—that is, their electronic connections to the world—is somehow *detrimental* to their education. So systematically, as kids enter our school buildings, we make them shut off all their connections. No cell phones. No music players. No game machines. No open Internet. When kids come to school, they leave behind the intellectual light of their everyday lives and walk into the darkness of the old-fashioned classroom. What are they allowed to use? Basal readers. Cursive handwriting. Old textbooks. Outdated equipment.

"Whenever I go to school," says one student I know, "I have to power down." He's not just talking about his devices—he's talking about his brain. Schools, despite our best intentions, are leading kids away from the light.

The Boredom Crisis

The reality is that students are, for the most part, bored. Pick an average kid, with an average schedule, and shadow him or her for a day in school—go where the student goes, sit in on all his or her classes—and see if *you* can stand it. Recently, at a conference of the heads of California's top independent schools, I asked a bright 10-year-old from one of the very best schools how often she's bored in class. "Ninety-nine percent of the time" was her immediate answer—she didn't even have to reflect. Even with the best teachers we have, most middle school and high school kids say they're bored 50–70 percent of the time.

And it makes perfect sense. A kid who has seen lunar landings and rovers working on Mars, who has done lots of research on the Internet on astronomy, and who comes to school excited about space travel may likely hear. "If you want to go to outer space, learn your math." But the math she learns is not about space—it's 1,200-year-old algebra and 4,000-year-old Egyptian geometry. A kid who has read and enjoyed the Harry Potter books must, in general, learn the rules of writing, spelling, and literary analysis not from the science fiction and fantasy books he enjoys, but from the books in the official curriculum. A kid who masters the electronic games Caesar III, Age of Kings, Age of Empires, Civilization IV, and Rise of Nations, and therefore knows a lot about world history, is likely to hear, "I don't know what's in those games, but the information may be incorrect. And besides, the history you should care about is what will be on the test."

School instruction is still mostly cookie cutter and one size fits all, despite the fact that we live in an era of customization— students continually customize their buddy lists, photos, ring tones, cell phone skins, Web sites, blogs, and MySpace and Facebook accounts. Moreover, with large class sizes and hundreds of kids to a counselor, schools are unlikely to be able to discover kids' passions and address their education from that base.

School Education Focuses on the Past

In the United States and other developed countries, education is quickly splitting into two separate—and unequal—parts. One part is "school," the education that kids, for the most part, are obliged to experience by law.

In exchange, school offers credentials—a diploma and a set of grades—that help determine students' future education and employment.

But many students find that schooling is almost entirely irrelevant to their present and future lives. For one thing, school is usually about the past—what we've learned up until this point (or some point a while ago) about math, science, language, and social studies—with, occasionally, a bit of current events thrown in.

School is certainly not about the future, which kids tell us is their most pressing concern. If schools were future oriented, they would be full of classes in programming, multimedia literacy and creation, astronautics, bioethics, genomics, and nanotechnology. Science fiction and fantasy literature would be a part

Virtual Classrooms Have Unique Benefits

Many schools are conducting classes in [the virtual online world] Second Life. Professors and students logon at a designated time and the professor conducts a class in Second Life. The premise of conducting classes online is to give students hands-on experience in the related field. It also encourages more participation and an exchange of ideas in a more casual, relaxed environment. In schools like USC's School of Engineering, classes are conducted to give students hands on experience for animation and modeling skills. The professors say that they want to give students exposure to what the industry is seeking from prospective graduates. The University of Hamburg uses virtual worlds where the virtual and reality are merged. A lecture taking place in a classroom is also attended by off-campus students via video streams and other media streamed to Second Life.

In addition to classes, virtual worlds can be used for virtual office hours and supplement traditional on-campus office hours. Students often find real-time office hours inconvenient and like the ability to interact with their instructors in a virtual setting at more convenient times.

Raymond Papp, "Virtual Worlds and
Social Networking: Reaching the Millennials,"
Journal of Technology Research, vol. 2,
September 2010.

of the curriculum, as representative of alternative visions of the future. Students would be learning and practicing such future-oriented skills as collaborating around the world electronically and learning to work and create in distributed teams.

Some educators justify the focus on the past by saying, "We don't even know what tomorrow's jobs will be—they haven't been invented yet." Perhaps. Yet we do know many, if not all, of tomorrow's needed skills—we're just not focusing on teaching them in school. Instead, school "covers material." It prepares kids for standardized exams. It continues to offer, for a ton of familiar reasons—such as No Child Left Behind, standards, and parent pressure—an outdated education that most students find irrelevant.

A Self-Taught Engagement with Current and Future Trends

There is another dimension to our kids' education that I call "after-school." After-school education is whatever the kids learn when they're *not* in class, doing their homework, or preparing for or taking tests. Some after-school learning—such as robotics clubs, competitions, and browsing in computer labs—takes place in our school buildings. But after-school learning goes much further. It encompasses all the time kids spend on the Internet at home. It includes all their blogging and social networking in MySpace or Facebook. After-school includes all the time kids spend sharing messages and pictures, talking on their cell phones, and creating many of the hundreds of thousands of videos posted on YouTube. It includes the time kids spend playing complex electronic games like Runescape and World of Warcraft and exploring online non-game worlds such as Whyville, Club Penguin, and Second Life, which are huge learning environments. After-school includes game and other computer programming classes that kids either sign up for or teach themselves. It includes an increasing number of noncurricular summer courses, learning camps, and other learning activities.

It's their after-school education, not their school education, that's preparing our kids for their 21st-century lives—and they know it. This after-school education doesn't bore them because, among other things, they help design it. It's different for every one of them. And there are no exams, only clear levels of competence that everyone knows and respects.

Preparing Kids for the Future

To make education relevant to students' lives and truly prepare kids for the future, we need to bring these after-school attractions into our schools. Four important practices can help.

Give students the opportunity to use technology in school. This is less about teachers mastering specific tools or techniques—such as electronic games, blogs, or search engines—than their being willing to allow students to use these tools to find information and create products. We vastly under-estimate our students' ability in technological areas and vastly inflate the threat of harm. These two perceptions have the combined effect of locking students in the past.

Some school districts have taken a different path. For several years, middle school students in Mabry, Alabama, have created 2- to 3-minute videos for a school "Oscars" program. The videos tackle such topics as immigration, adoption, physical fitness, homelessness, technology, and child labor. The judges, many of whom work in the communications and media industries, select winning films in such categories as best cinematography, best sound, best documentary, best dramatic comedy, and best teaching and learning film.

These are the kinds of products we should expect from our kids. Schools can address the "inappropriate use" issue, particularly in the higher grades, with one simple rule: If something comes on the screen that a student knows shouldn't be there, he or she has two seconds to shut off the computer—or lose all privileges.

Once we let students (particularly in groups) take the lead on technology projects, teachers tend to see more engagement and better results. As students share works in progress with the class for critical evaluation from both teacher and students, the teacher takes on the valuable roles of explainer, context provider, meaning maker, and evaluator/coach.

Find out how students want to be taught. This means devoting a meaningful amount of school time (and after-school time if possible) to conversing with students. It also involves promoting discussions on this topic among students, parents, teachers, and administrators. Such discussions might take the form of assemblies moderated, perhaps, by invited guests, such as a local law school professor with expertise at letting all groups have their say. Students would be invited to attend and contribute to the discussion. Both students and teachers have told me that in addition to using technology in school, students like having goals they want to reach, doing rather than listening, getting involved with the real world, having teachers ask them about their ideas and opinions, creating products that are important to them, and thinking seriously about their futures.

Connect students to the world. Today's students know that if they post something on YouTube, the entire world can see it—and comment. Many kids are in touch, through instant messaging, with friends and relatives around the world. So if students are studying the Middle East, why aren't they hooked up with Middle Eastern kids their own age? If they're learning Spanish, why aren't they connecting with kids in Latin America? If they're studying societies in social studies class, why aren't they exchanging videos showing their respective views of their own society?

Understand where kids are going—that is, into the future—and help them get there. "Most of us prefer to walk backward into the future," said management thinker Charles Handy, "a posture which may be uncomfortable, but which at least allows us to keep on looking at familiar things as long as we can." Covering the material and preparing kids for the test is not preparing them for the future. To find out the skills students need, look, for example, at the work of the Partnership for 21st Century Skills, which highlights such areas as computer and technology skills, critical thinking and problem solving, teamwork and collaboration, ethics and responsibility, and global awareness.

By engaging in these four practices, schools have a shot at being part of the "creatively preparing students for the future" process rather than just giving it up to after-school programs. To participate meaningfully in our kids' futures, schools must be willing, finally, to turn on the lights.

"Our public schools offer fewer and
fewer opportunities for civic discourse
and developing skills of debate,
negotiation, and critical thought."

The Millennial Generation
Desires a Change in Civic
and Political Discourse

Caitlin A. Baggott

*A renewed focus on civic discourse through the implementation
of new school programs and an emphasis on digital technologies
is necessary to help the Millennial generation realize their leadership potential and enact social change, argues Caitlin A. Baggott
in the following viewpoint. Baggott maintains that Millennials
crave open, honest discourse on issues such as race and inequality,
but they currently lack educational avenues to foster this change.
With the proper educational background, the author envisions a
multi-generational movement enacting the change that Millennials crave. Baggott is cofounder and director of education at the Or-
egon Bus Project, an organization that helps young people become
involved in the US democratic process.*

Caitlin A. Baggott, "If We Build It, They Will Come," *National Civic Review*, vol. 98, no. 3,
Fall 2009, pp. 30–33.

As you read, consider the following questions:

1. What three steps must be taken to improve Millennials' civic engagement?
2. How do Millennials feel about the current public dialogue about race, as stated by the author?
3. What do Millennials believe the role of the government should be, according to the June 2005 Democracy Corps poll cited by the author?

In early 2008, I was invited to deliver the commencement address at the Putney School, the small progressive private school in Vermont I had attended little more than a decade earlier. As the youngest speaker in the history of the school, I was invited to say something fairly obvious to the graduating seniors: "You/ we are the future." However, the headmaster pressed me to also say something else: "This generation feels the weight of the crisis in front of them acutely. Give them a reason to think that they can do it."

A Diverse Generation

This generation. Our generation. [President Barack] Obama would not have won without our votes. He wouldn't have gotten out of Iowa. We are about eighty to eighty-five million strong. In a handful of years we'll be 36 percent of the U.S. electorate. We're the largest and the most diverse generation in U.S. history, with almost 40 percent belonging to minority groups. We've been called generation Y, but most of us are happier with "millennial generation."

Twenty percent of us are immigrants or the children of immigrants. We were born sometime after the early 1980s and before the turn of the twenty-first century. We're nine years old, or suffering from acne and final exams in high school, or casting our first votes, sweating the 16 percent unemployment rate for people under thirty, seeking meaningful careers, and starting families. We're more likely than any previous generation to be the children of multiracial families. Nearly 90 percent of us believe it's OK for blacks and whites to date each other, a 30 percent increase over the same poll taken in 1987.

We are in a transformative age, and the millennial generation is both the recipient of that transformation and the final author of it. The magnitude of the change we're looking at is bigger than one black leader presiding in the Oval Office. Indeed, it would be a mistake to think that Obama's election was the catalyst for the deep civic interest and socially responsible focus that we see in the millennial generation. It might be more accurate to pin that laurel on public television, "Sesame Street," "Barney," and a concerted effort in our public schools to embrace multiculturalism.

Leadership Development Should Meet New Technologies

This is the generation I've been working with for about ten years now, as a teacher, organizer, and leadership coach. There are a lot of reasons to be hopeful, as the Putney School headmaster is, about the future of our country. However, the assumptions and expectations about racial equality and inclusion shared by this generation are not matched by our civic infrastructure.

Our public schools offer fewer and fewer opportunities for civic discourse and developing skills of debate, negotiation, and critical thought. Our models for creating inclusivity also embrace limitations and constraints that are no longer helpful. Our methods for developing leadership are overly hierarchical adaptations from our industrial past. Our definitions of civic participation have not kept up with modern communications technology. We must work rapidly and thoughtfully to meet this generation's leadership potential.

In the next two years, we need to support existing school-based, service-based, and leadership development programs, and create new ones to match a rising need.

Three Steps Necessary for Change in Civic Dialogue

First, we lack opportunities for open dialogue among peers (the face-to-face kind, not the "Tweeted" kind). Studies by the Center for Information and Research on Civic Learning and Engagement clearly show that these kinds of opportunities in middle and high school and college correlate directly and significantly with civic engagement, and they are often the first to get cut when school funding is on the chopping block.

Second, we need to continue to build and support opportunities for service. In 2009, the Obama administration increased funding for service through AmeriCorps (including programs such as Teach for America), tripling service positions for volunteers. Service leadership puts young leaders in a position to learn about community and government agencies, and to develop skills and ideas that prepare them to put their ideals into action.

Third, we need to create and support leadership development programs focused on next-generation leadership skills: collaboration, cross-cultural dialogue, team leadership, and service leadership. The traditional, top-down, crisis management leadership model will not function for this generation. The millennial generation already knows that the old models don't work, and their experiments with new leadership and decision-making models for campus organizing are giving them insights and ideas about how to lead community and legislative processes toward better, more inclusive public policy. However, they need more structured and clarified models for leadership from older and experienced community leaders—and need to be given the opportunity to test their new leadership models off campus.

Millennials Crave Honest Racial Debate

We also need to address inherited flaws and limitations in our approaches to race in our public discourse. The millennial generation craves open, courageous, humorous, and compassionate public dialogue about race, and on this front our elected leaders and the media are not keeping up with demand. During Obama's candidacy, race became a media focus in the late summer months, as the controversy over comments made by the Rev. Jeremiah Wright [whose church Obama attended] was heated by accusations from the right of reverse racism, anti-Americanism, and radical politics—then reheated and served up again by the mainstream media.

Jon Stewart's "Daily Show" handled the moment with a sketch in which Stewart couldn't put the "race genie" back in the bottle. For the millennial generation (and the "Daily Show" comedians) getting the genie back in the bottle is hardly the point. We millennials seek public leaders (and sketch comedians) who are willing to speak openly and candidly about what race has meant historically in America—and who have the capacity to imagine a more inclusive future. But the public dialogue about race is so constrained by uncertainty and orthodoxy that the millennials I work with end up feeling isolated or alienated.

I recently had the opportunity to witness and participate in a large-group conversation among college students, comparing Martin Luther King Jr.'s letter from Birmingham jail, [with] (then-candidate) Obama's speech addressing race in America, and the Rev. Wright controversy, "A More Perfect Union." The passionate and insightful conversation spanned more than an hour, exploring the differences and similarities in the arguments and styles of argument used by each man. But it was a simple rhetorical move of Obama's that sent a pulse of electricity through the room.

"Here Obama says, 'We don't talk about this stuff, but we must,'" one college student observed. "He's calling us to a national conversation about things that most people—most politicians particularly—brush under the rug."

Although the first part of the conversation was steady, academic, and polite, the topic of political honesty awoke something in the group. They interrupted each other and agreed with soft "yeses" and "mm-hmms."

Digital Technologies Hold the Potential for Civic Learning

It seems clear that many opportunities for meaningful civic learning exist in online environments using technologies that are familiar and appealing to digital natives, a term that Prensky coined to refer to people born after 1980 and coming of age with interactive, convergent digital media. Web 2.0—the style of internet programming that enables user-to-user contact, user expression, and user influence of website content—has understandable appeal for a young person. . . .

With respect to what kinds of engagement experiences are available online, it is clear that digital media and web networks offer great potential for reinvigorating youth participation. However, a large volume of intuitive and under-investigated generalizations stand in the way of clearly understanding how and when such potential may be realized, ranging from claims that experiences in video war games and popular culture fan sites are somehow civic, to the equally fervent convictions of designers and managers of youth engagement sites that their environments offer the kinds of civic experiences young people should have.

W. Lance Bennett, Chris Wells, and Allison Rank, "Young Citizens and Civic Learning: Two Paradigms of Citizenship in the Digital Age," Citizenship Studies, *April 2009.*

And then one student read from the text of Obama's speech, and the room grew still: We can pounce on some gaffe by a Hillary [Clinton, then Democratic presidential primary candidate] supporter as evidence that she's playing the race card, or we can speculate on whether white men will all flock to [Republican presidential candidate] John McCain in the general election regardless of his policies. We can do that. But if we do, I can tell you that in the next election, we'll be talking about some other distraction. And then another one. And then another one. And nothing will change. That is one option. Or, at this moment, in this election, we can come together and say, "Not this time."

Race Is Not the Only Issue of Concern

Our generation yearns for, and is beginning to create, forums to learn about and develop a new kind of political and civic discourse—a more honest and risk-accepting public speech. The old models of highly controlled public speech and public relations are no longer functional. The Internet, Facebook, Twitter, and the new nonmainstream news cycle means that political leaders need to learn how to act effectively in a media environment they cannot control in the same way that previous generations could.

In addition to opening space for political leaders to speak honestly about experiences of exclusion and injustice, we need to move toward a civic space in which leaders of color are asked to speak about public concerns that are not about race.

We need to create a new generation of multi-issue, multiconstituency organizations. We must move forward from the nonprofit infrastructure of the last four decades. In America, race and class have always been inextricably linked, and one of the frontiers for justice work in the coming decades is addressing economic disparities in the truly diverse impoverished white, black, Latino, and Asian Pacific Islander communities across the country. We need a multiracial movement to recalibrate economic injustice. The Green Jobs and alternative energy movements that have started during the last few years are a beginning, as are similar efforts for health care, education reform, and voter access.

In a June 2005 Democracy Corps poll, 63 percent of eighteen to twenty-nine-year-olds believed the role of government should be to "promote the principle of a strong community and policies that expand opportunity and promote prosperity for all, not just a few," compared to 35 percent who thought the role of government should be to promote the principle of self-reliance and policies of limited government and low taxes. Gen Xers, by contrast, were split 50 percent to 45 percent on this question.

Millennials show deep concern for today's income inequalities and social stratification. In the 2004 National Election Survey, 84 percent of millennials said that the gap between rich and poor had grown in the last twenty years and 94 percent thought that the change in the gap between rich and poor was a bad thing. These figures are higher than those for older generations. In the Magid Associates 2006 survey of millennials for the New Politics Institute, "transition" millennials (those born 1984–1988) were more likely than any other age group to favor governmental action to reduce economic differences among Americans.

Change Comes from All Generations

It is critical that the infrastructure we develop to support the millennial generation be explicitly multigenerational. Millennials are not unique for perceiving a new need for racial dialogue, community service, or new models of leadership. The rising tide of tolerance and inclusion is just as powerful a force for the "silent," baby boom, and gen X activists who spent the last several decades working toward this conclusion. Those of us born at the dawning of the Age of Aquarius aren't the only ones who experience these cultural changes; everyone does. We are inheriting a legacy of increasing inclusion and justness, and we want to learn from the successes and failures of those who came before us. We know from history that mass social movements are necessarily multigenerational. Those that don't look back for guidance and commit to pay it forward ultimately fail. However, we want to be invited as partners to this multigenerational dialogue—not students. We believe that we have experiences and insights that add value to the conversation.

America has a unique ability to absorb and digest change. Even the grandest pivots in culture, norms, policy, or inclination end in a shrug and a shuffle step. No big deal. People have been fighting, striving, pushing, resisting, struggling, marching, attesting and protesting, and organizing for generations. Change comes hard, and it costs blood, sweat, and tears; yet when it happens, it seems easy, choreographed, and inevitable. The change before us in the coming decades is not inevitable.

The radical and intentional efforts of the last several decades to raise a generation of Americans who live with race in a different way have been successful. As in that sappy 1990s classic film *Field of Dreams*, one generation has reached out to another by building a space for a new kind of civic performance—but this time reaching into the future, not the past. That admirable effort is not yet finished. But if we build it, they will come.

> "*The trouble with generational stereotyping is that it sucks the individuality out of our students.*"

Generational Stereotyping Inhibits Education

Mano Singham

In the following viewpoint, Mano Singham argues that generational stereotyping has led teachers to ignore their students' individual traits in favor of a general notion of the entire groups' characteristics. He maintains that this focus on select features, such as a need for instant gratification and clinginess to parents, has led educators to accept a universal definition of their students which could lead to less effective teaching. Singham believes that while generational stereotyping is well intentioned in an attempt to categorize changes to develop more effective teaching methods, it must be ended. Singham is a theoretical physicist and Director of the University Center for Innovation in Teaching and Education at Case Western Reserve University in Ohio.

Mano Singham, "More than 'Millennials': College Must Look Beyond Generational Stereotypes," *Chronicle of Higher Education*, vol. 56, no. 8, October 16, 2009, pp. A104. Copyright © 2009 by Mano Singham. All rights reserved. Reproduced by permission.

As you read, consider the following questions:

1. What are some of the characteristics of Millennial students as described by the professors at the college teaching conference referenced by Singham?
2. What examples of ethnic stereotypes are given by the author, and how do some professors react to these?
3. Instead of "a result of new traits emerging," Singham believes that the changes professors are observing have resulted from what other factors?

Until the 1990s, generations were thought by most people to span about 20 years, and labeling a generation with a catchy name usually meant that the cohort represented some major demographic trend. The births of the baby boomers, for example, had serious implications for social policy because of the need to project future needs in education, social services, and retirement. Giving that cohort an easily identifiable label made sense.

Now, however, it seems that a new generation is named every decade or less, driven by sweeping generalizations from the mass media and supported by little more than alleged changes in character traits as described by pop sociologists. One could dismiss all the generational splitting as the harmless fun of people in the news business, who need filler for their arts-and-style and pop-culture sections—except for the fact that it has seeped into academic conversations and may actually be influencing how we interact with college students, and not in a good way.

Defining and Redefining Generations

The first of the new breed of compressed generations was the so-called Generation X, consisting of those born after 1965, who are supposedly characterized by qualities of independence, resilience, and adaptability.

Tragically, before that generation could even reach its teenage years, it was killed off and replaced by Generation Y, consisting of those born after 1977. But it seems that Generation Y was unhappy with the label, and one can understand why. The letter X carries with it an aura of mystery, while Y is merely the letter after X, always playing second fiddle. Even in graphs, X is the independent variable, adventurously staking out new ground, while Y is the plodding dependent variable, following along in X's wake. Who wants to be part of that crowd? So Generation Y was rechristened as the Millennials, a catchy title for those coming of age at the turn of the century, and it has stuck.

And what do we know about these Millennials? A lot, it seems. Here's one description, from "Generation X and the Millennials: What You Need to Know About Mentoring the New Generations," by Diane Thielfoldt and Devon Scheef:

> The 75 million members of this generation are being raised at the most child-centric time in our history. Perhaps it's because of the showers of attention and high expectations from parents that they display a great deal of self-confidence. . . . Millennials are typically team-oriented, banding together to date and socialize. . . . They work well in groups, preferring this to individual endeavors. They're good multitaskers, having juggled sports, school, and social interests as children, so expect them to work hard. Millennials seem to expect structure in the workplace. They acknowledge and respect positions and titles, and want a relationship with their boss. . . . They are definitely in need of mentoring . . . and they'll respond well to the personal attention. Because they appreciate structure and stability, mentoring Millennials should be more formal, with set meetings and a more authoritative attitude on the mentor's part.

Really? We seem to have those 75 million people pegged, don't we?

The Millennial label was so successful that we were loath to let it go, so that generation was allowed to grow into adulthood until 1998, when the news media decided that it was time for a new one. Generation Z was thus born, comprising those born from the mid- to late-1990s through the 2000s. Their arrival is now indelibly linked with the events of September 11, 2001, and Generation's Z's worldview is supposedly shaped by that one event.

But that's not all. With the source of generation labels shifting from demographics to character traits and the influence of significant contemporaneous events, we have now gone back in time and cut earlier generations into more finely grained slices that encompass smaller age cohorts. Generation Next consists of people born between 1982 and 1989 who, according to the Pew Research Center, "have grown up with personal computers, cellphones, and the Internet and are now taking their place in a world where the only constant is rapid change." The MTV Generation consists of those who occupy the space between Generation X and Generation Y. Even the venerable baby boomers have succumbed to this generational Balkanization, with those born between 1954 and 1965 being peeled off and given their own enigmatic label of Generation Jones. Why? Because late boomers are presumed to have been too young to be deeply affected by the Vietnam War and Woodstock—supposedly the cultural touchstones that shaped the worldview of early boomers.

Generational Stereotypes Filter into Universities

I suspect that student-life and admissions administrators are the first to be influenced by such generational bandwagons. They have to deal with parents and with students' nonacademic lives, and thus must keep their antennae tuned to what is going [on] in popular culture. From them these terms diffuse into general university conversation.

I attended a conference on college teaching recently and was amazed at how often generational stereotypes were brought up and used as a valid basis for dealing with students. All it took was one person dropping the word "Millennial" into the discussion, and the anecdotes started pouring out: The students who demand instant gratification, those who send repeated e-mail messages to their professors in the middle of the night and are annoyed when they don't get an immediate reply, those who expect professors to give them a wake-up call on field trips because that is what their parents did, those whose parents cling to them and intercede on their behalf, those who cling to their parents, those who confide intimate details about their lives that professors need not (and would rather not) know, those who demand to be told exactly what they need to do on assignments, and so on. Such stories seem to spring from an inexhaustible well. And the picture of the Millennials that emerges is that of a whiny, needy, instant-gratification-seeking, grade-oriented bunch of students.

It should be borne in mind that those stories were not told by bitter, curmudgeonly, "you kids get off my lawn!"-type professors who hate being in the company of students and think that universities would be much better places if no pesky undergraduates were around to interrupt the day. The puzzle is that the people who attend such teaching conferences and make such comments are often some of the best and most caring teachers—the ones who are constantly trying to find ways to improve their teaching and reach more students.

The willingness of such professors to accept generational stereotypes stands in stark contrast to their sensitivity when it comes to gender and ethnic stereotypes. During one session on identifying and dealing with classroom incivilities, a couple of professors ventured the suggestion that what students considered uncivil may depend on their culture: that Korean students may unwittingly commit plagiarism because they believe that citing sources is an insult to their professor; that Saudi Arabian students like to negotiate grades with their professors because they come from a bargaining culture; that Latin American students think that something is cheating only if you get caught. There was immediate pushback from other professors that such generalizations are not valid—and are in fact harmful, because they prevent us from seeing the individuality in students. Generalizations about the Millennials, however, went unchallenged.

Accepting Generational Similarities Improves Education

A fact all have known for some time is that the abundance and convergence of new media is changing the structure of libraries and library service. However, adherence to generational differences as an underlying cause hinders educational pedagogy principally because we are all part of the current consumer-driven technology bubble. We are all part of "the Connected Generation." In many aspects, the core values of today's students are the same as their forefathers (community, integrity, love, competence, happiness, self-respect, and wisdom). Accepting this fact allows us to plan and accommodate for all groups well into the future. It allows us to focus on the individual learner and the learning itself without the brand label. It allows educators to understand that contemporary students follow time-honored consumer behavior in which choice and expediency (principle of least effort) is commonplace. Shedding reactionary differences allows educators to clearly focus on user education, connectivity, and seamless service. It allows educators to effectively see past the commodified student preoccupied more with life than education.

Charles H. Becker, "Student Values and Research: Are Millennials Really Changing the Future of Reference and Research?," Journal of Library Administration, *vol. 49, no. 4, June 2009.*

Generational Stereotypes Ignore Individual Behavior

Why are we in academe so accepting of media-driven constructs like the ever-multiplying generation labels? Paradoxically, it may be because we want to help students. Thoughtful academics are problem solvers, and when dealing with disengaged students, giving the problem a label gives one the sense that one understands it and can set about dealing with it.

But generational stereotypes are of no value for professors—and not because they are entirely false. After all, stereotypes are usually based on some reality. But even if different populations exhibit, on average, their own distinct traits, large populations like nations and generations include so many deviations from the norm that stereotypes are of little use in predicting the traits that any given person is likely to display.

It would be silly to argue that student behavior hasn't changed over time. But what we are observing may not be a result of new traits emerging, but rather old traits manifesting themselves in novel forms because of changes in external conditions. Maybe parents have not become more clingy or students more psychologically dependent on them. Perhaps the truth is simply that college has become vastly more complicated and difficult to navigate, with its explosion of majors, minors, and other programs—not to mention the byzantine rules for financial aid—so perhaps some parents have felt obliged to step in more than they might have in earlier generations to act on their children's behalf.

Similarly, we have always had students who were uninhibited, socially awkward, or needed instant gratification. But now e-mail and Facebook enable them to display those qualities in ways they couldn't before—such as by expecting immediate responses to midnight queries or revealing personal information online they should keep to themselves.

Teachers Must Have Affection for Their Students

Students are diverse and have always been diverse. I've taught for over three decades and have my own cache of funny or poignant stories about needy, annoying, or self-absorbed students. We teachers love stories about students, and treasure and accumulate them like anglers or golfers do about their pastimes. While my own stories can fit those spread around about the Millennials, many of them are about students from long ago, before it became fashionable to label students according to their birth years.

Bertrand Russell said that "no man can be a good teacher unless he has feelings of warm affection toward his pupils and a genuine desire to impart to them what he himself believes to be of value." The trouble with generational stereotyping is that it sucks the individuality out of our students, the very thing that generates those feelings of warm affection. It makes them into generic types, whose personalities and motivations we think we can discern without having to go to all the bother of actually getting to know them.

Periodical Bibliography

The following articles have been selected to supplement the diverse views presented in this chapter.

Benjamin Ola Akande	"The I.P.O.D. Generation," *Diverse: Issues in Higher Education*, September 4, 2008.
Jennifer Deal, David Altman, and Steven Rogelberg	"Millennials at Work: What We Know and What We Need to Do (If Anything)," *Journal of Business and Psychology*, June 2010.
Dianne Durkin	"Youth Movement," *Communication World*, March–April 2008.
Douglas L. Keene and Rita R. Handrich	"Between Coddling and Contempt: Managing and Mentoring Millennials," *Jury Expert*, September 2010.
Alec Levenson	"Millennials and the World of Work: An Economist's Perspective," *Journal of Business and Psychology*, June 2010.
Graham Manville and Gill Schiel	"Generation Y is Wired up and Ready for Action so What's the Problem?," *Times Higher Education*, August 14, 2008.
Angela Provitera McGlynn	"Millennials in College: How Do We Motivate Them?," *Education Digest*, February 2008.
Nancy Sutton Bell, J.A. Connell, and Nathan E McMinn	"How Will the Next Generation Change the Business World? A Report on a Survey," *Insights to a Changing World Journal*, March 2011.
Andrew Trotter	"Scholars Diverge in Assessing the Intellect of 'Digital Kids,'" *Education Week*, October 8, 2008.
Patrick Tucker	"Teaching the Millennial Generation," *Futurist*, May–June 2006.

CHAPTER 3

What Social Factors Have Shaped the Millennial Generation?

Chapter Preface

The Millennial generation in the United States came of age at an unusual time. Though the wars in Iraq and Afghanistan have made the costs of military engagement clear to young people, this generation has grown up relatively threat-free. Certainly the September 11, 2001, terrorist attacks on US soil made Americans feel vulnerable, but the singularity of the incident only emphasizes the security the nation has otherwise enjoyed. Ashley Smalls, nineteen when she was interviewed in the *Huffington Post* on September 9, 2011, asserted that 9/11 "made me realize that the world isn't made of all sunshine and rainbows, that we have these enemies and that there's this hatred aimed directly at us." However, according to a survey of young people conducted by the American University School of Communication in April 2011, recognizing the momentousness of the event did not lead to lingering fears. According to the survey, more than 70 percent of those polled said they were "not too worried" or "not worried at all" that they or their relatives would become victims of terrorism. The Millennials will definitely not forget the impact of 9/11—the institution of airport security screenings is an ever-present reminder—but with few terrorist threats since 2001, young people have returned their attention to the demands of normal daily routines.

Perhaps more influential on the day-to-day lives of the Millennial generation is the fallout from the global economic crisis of 2008. With high unemployment still plaguing the country, and businesses cutting back on new hires, salary raises, and benefits, young people eager to start work may find it difficult to land the perfect job. In a May 17, 2011, post for *USA Today College*, Cryn Johannsen writes, "Millennials, with or without higher education, have been hit the hardest by the recession." She points out that young workers are fighting older, more experienced unemployed people for whatever positions become available. Johannsen cites an April 20, 2011, survey by the Economic Policy Institute that reveals the unemployment rate for workers age sixteen to twenty-four is 18.4 percent—about twice the national average and the worst on record for the past sixty years. Many Millennials remain optimistic that the economy will turn or that their schooling will help them find employment with a good salary, but so far the job environment has not yielded the opportunities young people expect. Some are stuck in low-paying, entry-level positions and expect to change jobs when the economy improves. A May 2011 survey by SBR Consulting found that 70 percent of Millennials claimed there is a "possibility" they would switch employers if there was an upturn (and 38 percent of those surveyed said they would jump ship because of the job they currently do).

The economic crisis and the legacy of September 11, 2011, are two influential events that have shaped Millennials' lives. In addition to the impact of current events, authors in the following chapter examine how the Millennial generation is affected by the ways previous generations have shaped society and business. Collectively, these writers address the fundamental question of how well-prepared this generation is to face a world shaped by forces not of their making.

> "Today, if you are thinking about
> standing on the shoulders of the past
> generation, I'd say 'Please don't.'"

The Millennial Generation Has Inherited Numerous Problems from the Baby Boomers

Mitchell E. Daniels Jr.

Mitchell E. Daniels Jr. is the Governor of Indiana. A Republican, Daniels was first elected in 2004 and won a second term in 2008. In the following viewpoint, a commencement speech given at Indiana's Butler University in 2009, Daniels suggests that the graduating class not follow in the footsteps of their predecessors, the Baby Boom generation. In Daniels's opinion, the Baby Boomers—of which he counts himself a member—have too often been frivolous, selfish, and generally unconcerned about public responsibility or civic welfare. Daniels urges the graduates—members of the Millennial generation—to become a more potent force in US history, one renowned for saving and planning for the future, and one that does not condone bad behaviors in business, government, or society.

As you read, consider the following questions:

1. For what "admirable" characteristic does Daniels think the Baby Boomers will be remembered in history?
2. Why does Daniels contend that increasing levels of Social Security and Medicare benefits are a reflection of Baby Boomer mentality?
3. Why does Daniels encourage the Butler graduates—and all Millennials—to "be judgmental?"

If you're like I was, and most college graduates I've known, you will soon look back and say "Wow, I got out of there just in time." It's a very human tendency to conclude that one's high school or college went straight to hell right after they left. It's typical to recall these years with increasing fondness and nostalgia, to think of them as special, and to imagine your class as the greatest the school has seen.

On the record so far, you are. Your entering SAT scores, and the difficulty of many of the courses you've just taken, surpass any in Butler [University] history. But the record of your class has only a first chapter; what counts is what you will do with your education, and your lives, starting—that is, *commencing*, tomorrow. Years from now, when you are addressing commencements or attending them as parents, people will review that collective record, and pronounce you either a good, an ordinary, or, who knows, maybe a great class. Of course, what really matters is what you do or don't achieve individually, but prepare to be lumped together in various ways and assessed as a group.

The Insidious Generation Generalization

Among the grossest and most arbitrary of such lumpings is the idea of a *generation*, a generalization at war with the obvious reality that any age cohort is widely diverse, containing heroes and villains, angels and devils, geniuses and fools. The parents here today are wonderful people, who have loved you, sacrificed for you, and taught you well. Neither you nor they would be here, if that were not so. But many of their peers made very different choices.

Even though the whole notion of a "generation" must be discounted as the loosest of concepts, within limits it is possible to spot the defining characteristics of an age and the human beings who create it. Along with most of your faculty and parents, I belong to the most discussed, debated and analyzed generation of all time, the so-called Baby Boomers. By the accepted definition, the youngest of us is now forty-five, so the record is pretty much on the books, and the time for verdicts can begin.

Which leads me to congratulate you in advance. As a generation, you are off to an excellent start. You have taken the first savvy step on the road to distinction, which is to follow a weak act. I wish I could claim otherwise, but we Baby Boomers are likely to be remembered by history for our numbers, and little else, at least little else that is admirable.

The Unfortunate Choices of the "Me Generation"

We Boomers were the children that the Second World War was fought for. Parents who had endured both war and the Great Depression devoted themselves sacrificially to ensuring us a better life than they had. We were pampered in ways no children in human history would recognize. With minor exceptions, we have lived in blissfully fortunate times. The numbers of us who perished in plagues, in famine, or in combat were tiny in comparison to previous generations of Americans, to say nothing of humanity elsewhere.

All our lives, it's been all about us. We were the "Me Generation." We wore t-shirts that said "If it feels good, do it." The year of my high school commencement, a hit song featured the immortal lyric "Sha-la-la-la-la-la, live for today." As a group, we have been self-centered, self-absorbed, self-indulgent, and all too often just plain selfish. Our current Baby Boomer President [Barack Obama] has written two eloquent, erudite books, both about . . . himself.

As a generation, we did tend to live for today. We have spent more and saved less than any previous Americans. Year after year, regardless which party we picked to lead the country, we ran up deficits that have multiplied the debt you and your children will be paying off your entire working lives. Far more burdensome to you mathematically, we voted ourselves increasing levels of Social Security pensions and Medicare health care benefits, but never summoned the political maturity to put those programs on anything resembling a sound actuarial footing.

In sum, our parents scrimped and saved to provide us a better living standard than theirs; we borrowed and splurged and will leave you a staggering pile of bills to pay. It's been a blast; good luck cleaning up after us.

In Christopher Buckley's recent satiric novel *Boomsday*, the young heroine launches a national grassroots movement around the proposal that Boomers should be paid to "transition", a euphemism for suicide, at age 75, to alleviate this burden. That struck me as a little extreme; surely 85 would do the trick. Buckley meant his book for laughs, of course, but you'll find nothing funny about the tab when it comes due.

Our irresponsibility went well beyond the financial realm. Our parents formed families and kept them intact even through difficulty "for the sake of the kids." To us, parental happiness came first; we often divorced at the first unpleasantness, and increasingly just gave birth to children without the nuisance of marriage. "Commitment" cramps one's style, don't you know. Total bummer.

A defining book of our generation was Tom Wolfe's *The Electric Kool-Aid Acid Test*, which chronicled the exploits of Ken Kesey and his Merry Pranksters, practitioners of the drug-taking '60s counterculture in its purest form. On the last page of the book, in a pseudo-intellectual, LSD-induced haze, Kesey chants over and over the phrase "We blew it."

In that statement, if in no other way, Kesey and his kind were prophetic.

Opportunities for Greatness

As time runs out on our leadership years, it's clear there is no chance that anyone will ever refer to us, as histories now do our parents, as "The Greatest Generation." There is no disgrace in this; very few generations are thought of as "great." And history is not linear. Many generations fail miserably at the challenges they confront, and their societies take steps backwards as a consequence. Consider Japan before World War II, or Americans in the decades before the Civil War.

And yet in both those instances and many others, the people who followed did great things, not only redeemed all the failings but built better, fairer societies than their nations had seen before. In fact, true greatness can only be revealed by large challenges, by tough circumstances. And your opportunities for greatness will be large.

Among the reasons I usually duck commencements is the danger of lapsing into clichés, and I'd bet that no cliché is more worn out on these occasions than the phrase "standing on the shoulders of giants." Like all such phrases, it was inventive and interesting when Sir Isaac Newton coined it, but centuries later it's overdue for retirement. In one commencement speech I read about, our current Secretary of State [Hillary Clinton] managed to use it twice in a single paragraph.

Today, if you are thinking about standing on the shoulders of the past generation, I'd say "Please don't." Of course, I don't mean for a moment that you should not appreciate profoundly the health, wealth, comfort, the great innovations, and the general absence of world conflict which make this age in this nation the luckiest that ever was. After all, "thankfulness" is a pillar of "The Butler Way."

The Responsibility to Do What Is Right

What I mean to suggest is that you take into the world the values written on the locker room wall at Hinkle, which are not much at all like those associated with the Baby Boom. That you live for others, not just yourselves. For fulfillment, not just pleasure and material gain. For tomorrow, and the Americans who will reside there, not just for today. That song I mentioned ends with the refrain, "And don't worry 'bout tomorrow, hey, hey, hey." When it comes on oldies radio, please, tune it out. Do worry 'bout tomorrow, in a way your elders often failed to do.

And please, just to revise another current practice, *be judgmental*. Whatever they claim, people always are, anyway—consider the healthy stigmatization of racist comments or sexist attitudes or cigarette smoking. It's just a matter of which behaviors enough of us agree to judge as unacceptable.

As free people, we agree to tolerate any conduct that does no harm to others, but we should not be coerced into condoning it. Selfishness and irresponsibility in business, personal finances, or in family life, are deserving of your disapproval. Go ahead and stigmatize them. Too much [of] such behavior will hurt our nation and the future for you and the families you will create.

Honesty about shortcomings is not handwringing. Again, this is a blessed land, in every way. Amidst the worst recession in a long time, we still are wealthier than any society in history. We are safer, from injury, disease, and each other than any humans that ever lived. Best of all, we are free. The problems you now inherit are not those of 1776, or 1861, or 1929, or 1941. But they are large enough, and left unattended, they will devour the wealth and, ultimately, the freedom and safety we cherish, at least in our thankful moments. So you have a chance to be a great Butler class, part of a great generation.

You're thinking, "Don't lay all that on me. My one life's plenty to take care of," and that's true. But if enough of you choose to live responsibly, for others, for tomorrow, the future will remember you that way, when it assesses you as a lump.

You are in fact off to a great start, provided, that is, that you absorbed a bit of the tradition around here. Here's a real, if apocryphal, story we were told at your age. It was said then that Butler recruiters would travel to high schools on the East Coast promising parents "Send your child to Butler and we will send them back the same person you raised."

Surely, if ever actually stated, that was never true. You are a very different person than you were on arrival, certainly wiser and more knowledgeable, which are two different things. I hope you are also more inclined to unity. To humility. To thankfulness. If so, you leave the lot fully loaded, equipped with all the standard features and the factory options, too. You're ready for the road.

And if enough of you drive carefully, and responsibly, one day on this hallowed wood floor some other soon-to-be-forgotten speaker will look back and say, "Oh, 2009. That was a great class. They were part of a great generation. They did it The Butler Way."

> "If Boomer parents have anything for which to be sorry it's for rearing a generation of pampered kids who've been chauffeured around to soccer leagues since they were 6."

This Boomer Isn't Going to Apologize

Stephen Moore

In the viewpoint that follows, Stephen Moore claims that the Baby Boom generation has been unfairly chastised for leaving a legacy of selfishness, greed, and environmental tragedy for today's Millennial generation. Moore argues that the Boomers actually cleaned up the environment and passed on more financial wealth to subsequent generations. He states that the sense of security and the luxuries the Millennials enjoy—indeed, expect—are the true heritage of the Boomers, and he chides young people for being ungrateful for these gifts. Stephen Moore is an economics writer for the Wall Street Journal *and a member of the Baby Boom generation.*

As you read, consider the following questions:

1. How do Millennials regard "rising affluence," according to Moore?

2. As reported by CBS and cited by the author, how much money do Millennials spend each year in the United States?

3. What is the net worth of the United States today, as Moore claims?

L ast weekend I attended my niece's high-school graduation from an upscale prep school in Washington, D.C. These are supposed to be events filled with joy, optimism and anticipation of great achievements. But nearly all the kids who stepped to the podium dutifully moaned about how terrified they are of America's future—yes, even though Barack Obama, whom they all worship and adore, has brought "change they can believe in." A federal judge gave the commencement address and proceeded to denounce the sorry state of the nation that will be handed off to them. The enemy, he said, is the collective narcissism of their parents' generation—my generation. The judge said that we baby boomers have bequeathed to the "echo boomers," "millennials," or whatever they are to be called, a legacy of "greed, global warming, and growing income inequality."

And everyone of all age groups seemed to nod in agreement. One affluent 40-something woman with lots of jewelry told me she can barely look her teenagers in the eyes, so overcome is she with shame over the miseries we have bestowed upon our children.

The *Wall Street Journal* reported last week that graduation ceremonies have become collective airings of guilt and grief. It's now chic for boomers to apologize for their generation's crimes. It's the only thing conservatives and liberals seem to agree on. Mitch Daniels, the Republican governor of Indiana, told Butler University grads that our generation is "just plain selfish." At Grinnell College in Iowa, author Thomas Friedman compared boomers to "hungry locusts . . . eating through just about everything." Filmmaker Ken Burns told this year's Boston College grads that those born between 1946 and 1960 have "squandered the legacy handed to them by the generation from World War II."

I could go on, but you get the point. We partied like it was 1999, paid for it with Ponzi schemes and left the mess for our kids and grandkids to clean up. We're sorry—so sorry.

Well, *I'm* not. I have two teenagers and an 8-year-old, and I can say firsthand that if boomer parents have anything for which to be sorry it's for rearing a generation of pampered kids who've been chauffeured around to soccer leagues since they were 6. This is a generation that has come to regard rising affluence as a basic human right, because that is all it has ever known—until now. Today's high-school and college students think of iPods, designer cellphones and $599 lap tops as entitlements. They think their future should be as mapped out as unambiguously as the GPS system in their cars.

CBS News reported recently that echo boomers spend $170 billion a year—more than most nations' GDPs—and nearly every penny of that comes from the wallets of the very parents they now resent. My parents' generation lived in fear of getting polio; many boomers lived in fear of getting sent to the Vietnam War; this generation's notion of hardship is TiVo breaking down.

How bad can the legacy of the baby boomers really be? Let's see: We're the generation that spawned Microsoft, Intel, Apple, Google, ATMs and Gatorade. We defeated the evils of communism and delivered the world from the brink of global thermonuclear war. Now youngsters are telling pollsters that they think socialism may be better than capitalism after all. Do they expect us to apologize for winning the Cold War next?

College students gripe about the price of tuition, and it does cost way too much. But who do these 22-year-old scholars think has been footing the bill for their courses in transgender studies and Che Guevara? The echo boomers complain, rightly, that we have left them holding the federal government's $8 trillion national IOU. But try to cut government aid to colleges or raise

Survey Finds the Baby Boomers Are Believed to Be More Productive and Less Self-Indulgent than Millennials

Which of the following generations would you say is the most productive?

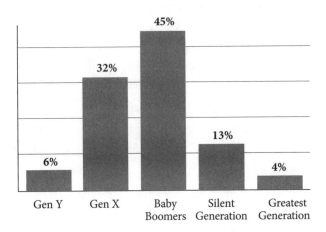

Which of the following generations would you say is the most self-indulgent?

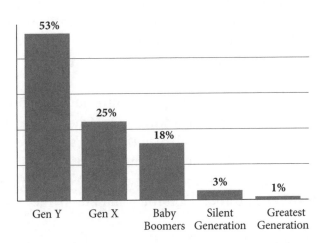

TAKEN FROM: Harris Interactive Survey for Charles Schwab and Age Wave, "Rethinking Retirement: Four American Generations Share Their Views on Life's Third Act," July 2008. www.agewave.com.

tuitions and they act as if they have been forced to actually work for a living.

Yes, the members of this generation will inherit a lot of debts, but a much bigger storehouse of wealth will be theirs in the coming years. When I graduated from college in 1982, the net worth of America—all our nation's assets minus all our liabilities—was $16 trillion, according to the Federal Reserve. Today, even after the meltdown in housing and stocks, the net worth of the country is $45 trillion—a doubling after inflation. The boomers' children and their children will inherit more wealth and assets than any other in the history of the planet— that is, unless Mr. Obama taxes it all away. So how about a little gratitude from these trust-fund babies for our multitrillion-dollar going-away gifts?

My generation is accused of being environmental criminals— of having polluted the water and air and ruined the climate. But no generation in history has done more to *clean* the environment than mine. Since 1970 pollutants in the air and water have fallen sharply. Since 1960, Chicago, Houston, Los Angeles and Pittsburgh have cut in half the number of days with unsafe levels of smog. The number of Americans who get sick or die from contaminants in our drinking water has plunged for 50 years straight.

Whenever kids ask me why we didn't do more to combat global warming, I explain that when I was young the "scientific consensus" warned of global *cooling*. Today's teenagers drive around in cars more than any previous generation. My kids have never once handed back the car keys because of some moral problem with their carbon footprint—and I think they are fairly typical.

The most absurd complaint of all is that the health-care system has been ruined by our generation. Oh, really? Thanks to massive medical progress in the past 30 years, the chances of dying from heart disease and many types of cancer have been cut in half. We found effective treatments for AIDS within a decade. Life expectancy has risen and infant mortality fallen. That doesn't sound so "selfish" to me.

Yes, we are in a deep economic crisis today—but it's no worse than what we boomers faced in the late 1970s after years of hyper-inflation, sky-high tax rates and runaway government spending. We cursed our parents, too. But then we grew up and produced a big leap forward in health, wealth and scientific progress. Let's see what this next generation of over-educated ingrates can do.

"*Millennials . . . cite the attacks on 9/11 as the most important influence shaping the attitudes and beliefs of our generation.*"

The 9/11 Terrorist Attacks Had a Significant Impact on the Millennial Generation

Eleni Towns

Eleni Towns is a research assistant with the Faith and Progressive Policy Initiative at the Center for American Progress, a progressive, public policy institute. In the viewpoint that follows, Towns recalls how many members of the Millennial generation were fraught with feelings of fear and patriotism in the immediate aftermath of the September 11, 2001, terrorist attacks. However, Towns reports that since that brief period of shock, Millennials have shown a great deal of tolerance and interest in expanding the United States' global partnerships in an effort to overcome the fear and work toward peaceful solutions to international relations. She claims that unlike older generations who experienced the 9/11 tragedy, young people are less Islamophobic, less eager to engage terrorism with military force, and more willing to become civically active to help the nation at home and improve the United States' international reputation.

As you read, consider the following questions:

1. How does Millennial patriotism seem to differ from that of older generations, according to Towns?
2. As the author reports, what percent of Millennials say they would be unwilling to join the US military?
3. By what percent has the academic study of religion increased in the last decade, as Towns writes?

My first day of high school was September 11, 2001. In an all-school assembly, a teacher stood to break the news and explain the significance of the attacks. His somber tone frightened us and as we were dismissed I clung to my friends out of fear and complete confusion. In the 10 years since, I have learned that my experience was typical of most in my generation. Across the country young people were in school when the attacks happened—some in elementary school, others in high school or college—and 9/11 literally became part of our education.

This Sunday [September 11, 2011], America will pause to remember those lost on that day and to reflect on how the country has changed over the last decade. The millennial generation—those who came of age during this time and have grown up in a post-9/11 America—possess unique insights and views based on our place in history.

Millennials in a 2009 [Center for American Progress (CAP)] survey cite the attacks on 9/11 as the most important influence shaping the attitudes and beliefs of our generation. But what lessons have we learned and how might those who will become our future leaders implement these lessons as we chart the course of our country in the years ahead?

While our generation is still forming our views, there are a few ways in which we have already grown. Below is a snapshot of recent polling of our views. CAP also reached out to a diverse group of millennials to document our memories, our lessons learned, and our hopes for the futures and are captured in the video "Millennial: Growing up in a Post-9/11 World." Some of these thoughts are also included below.

Defining the Millennial Generation

Millennials—generally classified as those who [were] born between 1978 and 2000—make up America's largest generation. Depending on how the parameters are set, we are as much as 30 percent larger than the Baby Boomers. We are also the most racially and ethnically diverse generation in U.S. history—61 percent are white, 19 percent Hispanic, 14 percent black, and 5 percent Asian. Millennials are also the most diverse generation in terms of place of birth and religion.

Millennials are also well connected through social media. Often dubbed the Facebook generation, 83 percent of young people utilize social media and other internet-based communication tools to easily connect with our fellow Americans and our communities. Millennials are more likely to identify as Democrats and hold traditional progressive values about economic and social inequalities, belief in government, and multilateral foreign policy.

From Patriotism to Civic Engagement

Immediately following the September 11 attacks, a wave of patriotism swept the nation. Citizens volunteered their time and blood to help those in need in New York City and Washington, D.C. And across the nation, Millennials witnessed—and took part in—the immediate unity that often arises in times of crisis and uncertainty. Our parents displayed flags on cars, in shop windows, and homes. Teachers and educational institutions, from grade schools to universities, set up informal and more structured discussions about the impact of the attacks and what it meant to be American. Many of our leaders spoke of the resiliency and strength of the union.

On May 2 of this year, when the death of [terrorist mastermind of the attacks] Osama bin Laden was announced, many

Millennials took to the streets to display similar signs of patriotism. From gatherings in front of the White House to campuses [from] Indiana State to Boston University, students waved flags and chanted "USA." For many, bin Laden was the generational villain and his death, if only symbolically, was a victory for America.

In the years between 2001 and 2010, however, Millennials have expressed a kind of patriotism that tends to be different from our elders. For example, polls show that far fewer young Americans than older ones believe it is unpatriotic to criticize leaders during war. Millennials, compared to older generations, believe more in the role of government and are far less skeptical of government.

Millennial patriotism has translated into increased civic engagement and volunteerism. UCLA's annual American Freshman survey found that volunteerism is unusually high among the generation. Eighty-three percent of entering freshman in 2005 volunteered during high school, 71 percent on a weekly basis. We are also more politically engaged. In both the 2004 and 2008 elections, there were significant increases in voters between the ages of 18 and 29.

Fear and Its Impact on Civil Liberties

In the 10 years since 9/11, America has justified, in the name of security, the limitation of civil liberties through policies such as the Patriot Act. Immigration policy has also become more restrictive and entry lists are increasingly backlogged for families, workers, and refugees.

Millennials have lived most of our adult lives in this world of increased security measures. Very few remember a time before the existence of the Transportation Security Administration or when family could pick up passengers at the gate after a flight. Color-coded threat levels and signs along interstate highways, as well as on buses and metros, that say "if you see something, say something" have become commonplace reality.

A Defining Moment for Millennials

9/11 was a fire that shaped a generation. It's true that Americans of all ages felt shock, fear, and uncertainty at attacks unlike any the nation had experienced. But for young people, the events of that day were a defining epic, in the way that Pearl Harbor and John F. Kennedy's assassination were for their elders.

For many it was the first time they'd seen adults cry; the first time they'd felt their security threatened; the first time the outside world had reached through the television screen and tapped them on the shoulder, figuratively speaking.

Peter Grier, "How 9/11 Has Shaped a Generation of Americans," Christian Science Monitor, *September 9, 2011.*

Millennials, however, see alternatives to these measures. A plurality do not believe we need to compromise civil liberties in order to protect the United States from terrorism. Millennials are also less accepting of racial profiling—as documented by recent Pew polling that found we are less supportive of extra airport checks on people who appear to be of Middle Eastern descent. And Millennials are much less supportive of further restrictions on immigration than older generations. Many spoke of the blinding impact of fear. Peter Nyger, age 28, believes that in the last 10 years "instead of embracing our liberties, [America] sacrificed them in the hopes of a safer society."

This isn't to say that the Millennials are immune to security fears or that we do not feel vulnerable to future terrorism. Harleen Gambir, age 18, shared the vulnerability she felt living in [the] post-9/11 world. "Dealing with this new reality is something that our generation is going to have to deal with. From now on there is never going to be a complete defeat of the people who want to harm us." Nearly 85 percent of respondents in a Brookings survey of Millennials said they couldn't envision a point in their lives when terrorism would no longer be a danger. Yet we tend to view the balance between security and other issues differently than our elders. In the same study, while Millennials cited terrorism as the most important future challenge, they also gave top priority to climate change, nuclear proliferation, and global poverty.

Thinking Globally

Fear or anger hasn't sent the Millennial generation into seclusion, despite the fact many Millennials believe that the U.S. is no longer globally respected. In fact, Millennials, in spite of or in response to the 9/11 attacks, are more eager than our predecessors to engage with other cultures firsthand and some have embraced opportunities to be a more global generation. Nick, age 26, felt 9/11 was the catalyst that incorporated the generation into a global society. "It's the event that connected us to the rest of the world . . . We learned to look at ourselves differently as an actor on the world's stage, and not just as an individual nation."

Millennials are reaching out to cultures abroad. More Millennials study abroad compared to previous generations and interest in nontraditional destinations has grown as more students study outside of Western Europe. In only the first academic year following 9/11, participation in [study] abroad programs jumped 8.8 percent. Although many expected study abroad participation to Islamic countries to drop after 9/11, enrollment rose 127 percent from 2002 to 2006, according to studies from the Institute of International Education.

Scholarship of foreign languages has also diversified. Due to federal government incentive programs and a general increase in curiosity, more students learn Arabic, Persian, Urdu, Punjabi, Turkish, Indonesian, Hindi, and Bengali than in the past. This trend isn't unprecedented. In response to the Cold War, government supported language studies led 30,000 or more American university students to Russians courses each year. Regardless of the incentive, however, the increased exposure to the Middle East, North Africa, and to the 1.2 billion person Muslim world by America's young people is sure to influence the country in the years to come.

Although our generation has lived most of our adult lives in a country at war, we have a different experience with military service than previous generations. Just 2 percent of Millennial males are military veterans. In comparison, 6 percent of the Generation X men and 13 percent of Baby Boomer men were veterans at comparable stages of their life cycle.

While Millennials consider themselves patriotic, according to 2007 polling, almost 70 percent say they would be unwilling to join the U.S. military. In fact, in general, Millennials are more likely to reject the primacy of military force in fighting terrorism or keeping America safe. Millennials share a more progressive stance on international affairs, oriented toward a multilateral and cooperative foreign policy. The generation is less supportive of remaining in Iraq and Afghanistan.

Tolerance of Diversity

Since 9/11, attitudes toward Muslims and Islam have become more negative. At the same [time] efforts to increase knowledge of the religion have also increased. Millennials are less accepting of the first trend and more engaged in the second.

Anti-Islam sentiment spiked in the year following 9/11 and has jumped again in the last two years. Today, local communities fear the building of mosques, states question the practice of Sharia, and political dialogue and election rhetoric is increasingly inflammatory and Islamophobic. Younger Americans are much more sensitive to this unequal treatment of Muslims. Forty-eight percent of Millennials believe Muslims are unfairly targeted compared to 27 percent of adults age 65 or older who believe the same thing. Younger people are also much more knowledgeable of Muslims and Islam, more tolerant of religious diversity, and of immigrants in general. The young, according to a Pew poll released last week, are roughly twice as likely to be troubled by the fact that Muslims are singled out for increased government surveillance and monitoring.

Many of these trends can be attributed to a natural curiosity and a concerted educational campaign that has given rise to more education about Islam and Muslim-majority cultures in the last 10 years. In many ways, Millennials have been the recipients, through our elementary and university classrooms, of this increased intercultural and interfaith education.

The study of religion has increased 22 percent in the last decade, according to the American Academy of Religion. Similar increases have occurred in the number and diversity of religion-related degrees offered. Between 2000 and 2005 alone, the number of college courses on Islam and Hinduism nearly doubled. Religion departments have expanded across the country from University of Texas to Ohio State and Georgia State.

This increased interest in religious scholarship and Islam is a promising sign for the future as polls reveal that those who are more educated about Islam and Muslims are also more tolerant of Muslim Americans.

In fact, this year [2011] more than 400 college campuses accepted President Barack Obama's Interfaith and Community Service Campus Challenge, committing to a year of interfaith service and programming on campus.

Millennials Are Already Influencing U.S. Policy

Millennials are patriotic and believe in America's institutions and the democratic process, which demands civic participation and the ability of free speech, even against leadership. The generation is also more tolerant and welcoming of different people and more eager to engage in the world beyond our borders.

Why is it important to examine what Millennials have learned from the 9/11 attacks and America's response to it? It is clear that Millennials will one day govern the country, but our impact on America occurs long before we take the reins of leadership. In the 2016 presidential elections, Millennials will make up at least one-third of the eligible voter electorate. How this generation views the world and America's polices 15 years after 9/11 will no doubt influence our choice of leadership. This anniversary we can begin to see how these worldviews are forming.

"In the space of 10 years, as the high schoolers and college students who lived through 9/11 grew into adulthood, some say the fire and death of that day have lost some of their potency."

The Impact of 9/11 on the Millennial Generation Has Lessened over Time

Joan Garrett

In the following viewpoint, Joan Garrett, a staff writer for the Chattanooga Times Free Press, *claims that while the terrorist attacks of September 11, 2001, had an immediate impact on the nation, the anxiety many people felt has faded over time. Garrett writes that for the Millennial generation, the pressing daily concerns of job insecurity, educational pursuits, and family life have overshadowed panic over terrorist threats. Garrett also points out that the lack of subsequent attacks and the relative security of the nation have helped Americans feel safer and move on with their lives. However, Garrett recognizes that the shadow of 9/11 is still a significant force in the lives of many people who warn that the country should not fail to learn lessons from the tragic event.*

As you read, consider the following questions:

1. According to Garrett, which Americans are more likely to be reminded of the terrorist attacks of 9/11 even ten years after the event?
2. How has the visual media influenced the United States' memory of the 9/11 attacks, as Garrett suggests?
3. According to the people Garrett interviewed, why is it dangerous to forget 9/11?

People said 9/11 would change everything, and didn't it?

At the airport, we submit to full-body scans, take our shoes off and keep containers of liquids small enough to fit into Ziploc bags. We know words like Quran and Taliban. More of us have neighbors or sons and daughters who have come home from combat in Afghanistan or Iraq, and many know soldiers who never returned.

And there are the things we didn't see: warrantless wiretapping, our nation's marred image in the eyes of the rest of the world, a crushing debt caused, in part, by running two wars that cost billions of dollars each week.

Then there are things we think we've seen too much of: 6,000 U.S. soldiers killed overseas and more than 4,000 injured.

Other Issues Are More Pressing than 9/11

After the Twin Towers fell in New York City on Sept. 11, 2001, scholars and talking heads on cable news and radio said the day would define a generation, as the assassination of President John F. Kennedy or attack on Pearl Harbor did. It would be a day seared into the consciousness of the generation. Bumper stickers and signs read "Never forget."

But in the space of 10 years, as the high schoolers and college students who lived through 9/11 grew into adulthood, some say the fire and death of that day have lost some of their potency.

Real life got in the way and, for better or worse, the effects of 9/11 are more of an undercurrent than a surface wave.

For the 18- to 30-year-olds in the Tennessee Valley, talk of layoffs and double-dip recessions stirs more panic than terrorism these days. Nationally, the politics of war, privacy and security are forever altered, but it's hard to say how those debates reach those who live hundreds of miles from New York without military connection or political involvement.

For the bank teller who drives her young kids to school then soccer, for the senior in college looking to start a life and get a job, for the cable repairman going to night school, the imprint of 9/11 is not as glaring in daily life.

Drew Holland, a 25-year-old living in Hixson, said he still ties his shoes the same and eats three meals a day.

"I don't feel unsafe or safer than I did before," he said. "I'm sure there are things that have changed on a daily basis, but not that I think about."

Growing Accustomed to the Tragedy

The closer you were to the attack, the more you felt it. New Yorkers are reminded constantly by an altered skyline. The memory is closer to the surface for people in Washington, D.C., near where a plane hit the Pentagon, and in Pennsylvania, where the heroic efforts of passengers drove Flight 93 into a field instead of the White House.

Many live without people they loved and still grieve. First responders live with illnesses they got from hauling debris from the pit and from memories that never die.

Even here, the wreckage of that day jarred some enough to veer the direction of their lives.

There have been a lot of assumptions about how 9/11 would impact a generation of youth, but it's guesswork, said Christopher Horn, a 37-year-old political science professor at the University of Tennessee at Chattanooga. This fall, he is teaching a class on the

Millennial Generation, which covers 18- to 29-year-olds and also is known as Generation Y.

It's hard to point to reputable research that says this generation is more fearful or more engaged than previous generations and even harder to link changes to 9/11, he said.

"So much of what has been written is impressionistic. There has been a long-standing tendency to stereotype younger generations in similar ways, and that is mostly what is going on now," Horn said.

As a 27-year-old graduate student on 9/11, Horn said his sense of security was rattled for the first time. He was expecting his first child and called the days following the terrorist attack scary and uncertain. He rarely, if ever, thinks of that time now.

"I have accepted it as normal," he said.

That's also what his students told Horn this semester when they talked about the mark of 9/11. The freshmen in his class say the thought that bad things can happen to this country always has felt normal.

But there is a tinge of guilt about this, especially among those in their late 20s or early 30s who were old enough to understand the magnitude of the worst foreign attack on U.S. soil since Pearl Harbor in 1941.

When the anniversary approaches and the television is peppered with documentaries about survivors and Ground Zero, many are reminded that nearly 3,000 people died, that some people jumped from flaming towers to escape burning to death, that buildings collapsed, crushing others underneath. A barrage of images forces us to grow accustomed to the shock and ugliness.

"You always hate to get conditioned to think, 'Well, that is just how things are now,' but you kind of have to move on," said Jamie Hamby, a 32-year-old who lives in Cleveland, Tenn.

The grieving period can begin to come to an end, some say. After all, [terrorist mastermind of the 9/11 attacks] Osama bin Laden was caught and shot to death this year [2011], and we have been safe inside our borders from outside terrorists for a decade.

"We learn to live and we learn to move on because that is what's meant to happen," said Adrienne Teague, 27, who lives in downtown Chattanooga. "Where would we be if we constantly sat around mourning about it?"

The Risks of Forgetting

But holding tight to memories of that day is important to others, who say the attack has lived in the background of their lives all these years. They are the ones who will say, while it's easy to forget, losing a connection to 9/11 is dangerous.

Holly Vincent was recruiting at a college fair for Tennessee Tech University when she heard two planes had crashed in New York City.

At 24, she was newly wed to a Marine and felt terrified he would be called away as she watched the military recruiters pack up at the fair. They moved so fast, she said, it felt they were going to war that instant. In that moment, she decided she wasn't going to be a college recruiter anymore.

"It changed my whole perspective on life," said Vincent, a 34-year-old Cleveland resident who now works in public relations. "I didn't want to be in a hotel away from my family."

Her husband's commitment to the Marines was extended for a year because of 9/11, and every day she waited for news that he would be called away. It never came.

"I was scared to death," she said. "We had big plans. This was supposed to be a new chapter in our life."

William Lunny was just 16 when it happened. He calls the day "our big moment," and said it solidified his decision to join the military six years later.

Now, as a 26-year-old, he said he doesn't get tired of the anniversaries or memorial services, even though he notices fatigue in others his age or younger.

People don't like to dwell on what they can't control; they think about what is right in front of them, he said. But he wishes that weren't true.

There are still two wars going on. There still will be Tennessee families who lose loved ones because of the aftermath of that day, he said.

"You have to memorialize. If you don't learn history, you are doomed to repeat it. If we don't remember it, it was a waste," he said.

Periodical Bibliography

The following articles have been selected to supplement the diverse views presented in this chapter.

Ronald Brownstein et al.	"Children of the Great Recession," *National Journal*, May 8, 2010.
Christine Dugas	"'Generation Y' Faces Some Steep Financial Hurdles," *USA Today*, April 23, 2010.
Economist	"Generation Y Goes to Work," January 3, 2009.
Brittany Hite	"Employers Rethink How They Give Feedback," *Wall Street Journal*, October 13, 2008.
Sharon Jayson	"Will 9/11 Define a Generation?," *USA Today*, September 11, 2006.
Steve Maich	"Is This the Future? Don't Bet on It," *Maclean's*, December 1, 2008.
Laurie Penny	"Smile till It Hurts," *Soundings*, Summer 2010.
Anna Quindlen	"Stepping Aside," *Newsweek*, May 11, 2009.
Cindy Waxer	"Clash of the Generations," *Computerworld*, February 16, 2009.

CHAPTER 4

How Will the Millennial Generation Impact the Future?

Chapter Preface

A February 2010 poll from the Pew Research Center attempted to capture the prevalent attitudes of the Millennial generation in the United States. According to the poll, Millennials are more ethnically and racially diverse than previous generations and are expected to have more education than older adults. They are less religious and lean toward liberal political views. They are adept with technology, and 75 percent indicated they had a presence on a social networking website. The Pew survey, as well as other surveys, found that Millennials are optimistic about the future and expect to find meaningful ways to contribute to society. Speaking about the survey to NPR on February 24, 2010, Pew Research Center President Andrew Kohut said of the Millennials, "They're very confident that it's all going to work out in the end. Sixty-eight percent of them say either now or at some time in the future—mostly some time in the future—they will earn enough money to lead the kind of life they want."

With their largely-progressive politics and their confidence, Millennials are anticipated to be a force of change in the nation and the world. Andrea Stone, writing in *USA Today* on April 14, 2009, argues that young people are more civic-minded than other more-recent generations. She attributes this both to the focus on community and tolerance following the September 11, 2001, terrorist attacks and to the numerous causes that have found a home on social networking sites. Stone reports that both Teach for America and the Peace Corps have seen increased enrollment in recent years because of this desire to make a difference. Alan Solomont, the chairman of the Corporation for National and Community Service, told Stone that members of the Millennial generation are volunteering in large numbers and have responded to disasters such as Hurricane Katrina by physically taking action to help those in need. "They want to get things done, to fix things," Solomont stated, "They're not into chasing their own ideologies as much as rolling up their sleeves and improving things."

Stone and others have pointed out that today's young people are more connected to the rest of the world than previous generations. Whether because they have travelled outside the United States (70 percent of Millennials have, according to Stone) or because they share cyberspace with people from all over the world, this generation is uniquely in touch with a variety of cultures. Because of the recession in the United States, some are even looking for jobs in foreign markets, seemingly unafraid to make such a life-changing commitment. It remains to be seen, however, whether the interaction will lead to greater understanding of global problems and a pledge to fix those as well as domestic ailments.

In the chapter that follows, several analysts and commentators offer their views on how the Millennial generation will impact the future of the world. Some suggest US youth are already altering old attitudes and prejudices at home; others believe the "can do" spirit and the openness to global citizenship will also help this generation mend fences around the world. In a piece for the *Huffington Post* on October 10, 2011, David D. Burstein, an activist and executive director of Generation 18 (a voter registration booster organization), concluded, "There are hardly any problems today that aren't global problems from the environment to the economy—our world is becoming more and more interdependent. We can only confront these issues globally and in solidarity, and where our older leaders have failed, millennials are joining hands across the world to step up to the plate."

| *"Millennials are ready to start acting today. In fact we've already started."*

What Happens When Millennials Come Together

David D. Burstein

In the following viewpoint, David D. Burstein, a writer and activist, insists that the Millennial generation is ready and eager to face global problems and work together to create solutions. According to Burstein, young people are already gathering in international summits to discuss pressing issues, and some youth-oriented organizations have already taken action to redress wrongs and fight for good causes. Burstein notes that one advantage these young people have is that they know how to use modern communication networks to organize and, by employing these tools, can generate fresh approaches to problems.

As you read, consider the following questions:

1. How many countries does Burstein claim were represented at the One Young World conference in 2011?
2. Who is Oscar Morales, as Burstein describes him?
3. Why does the author think it is important that Millennials conceive of themselves as global citizens?

Crises are everywhere we turn, leaders have abdicated their responsibilities around the globe, and by most objective standards there is a huge mess growing bigger and bigger that is being left for my generation—the millennial generation—to clean up. This generation is ready to step up to the challenge. We're eager to solve problems and address challenges in our communities, countries, and around the world.

We're a generation of pragmatic idealists, eager to bring about big change, but realizing it can only be done with a pragmatic approach. Politicians like to use the phrase "we have to do this for the young people" as a way to urge their fellow politicians to act, but the millennials are ready to start acting today. In fact we've already started.

Millennials have been organizing online and offline for years, but more and more they are gathering specifically to try and tackle these problems. They were brought together in this way just a few weeks ago at the second edition of a conference called One Young World in Zurich, Switzerland. Over 1200 young people from 170 countries, including countries often underrepresented at global gatherings like Iran, Libya, Iraq, Egypt, Tunisia, and Saudi Arabia, all came together ready to share, collaborate and solve.

There's an overabundance of conferences, summits, and self-described world-changer clubs. And I've been to many of them . . . But I think many of them could be replaced with this one. Did the conference end in solutions to all our world's problems? No. But two things made this event valuable to the 1200 young people who participated and potentially to the world. It is truly the only global youth summit, and the only one that brings together not just leaders but also regular citizens. The mere act of young leaders and citizens from all over the world, meeting, connecting, and working in concert, could tip the balance of some of our most pressing global challenges.

One Young World is representative of something I think we'll see a lot more of (whether organized or informal). This generation has come of age in a rapidly globalizing world. We're comfortable with it and we are excited about it. In the wake of the tenth anniversary of 9/11, there has been a great deal of discussion about the impact of the attacks on the millennial generation, the climate of fear it created. But while many of our older counterparts reacted to these events by becoming isolationist, millennials have embraced the need to globalize, and have become the first generation of truly global citizens. We're the first generation to spend all of our grown years in a world where connecting to people from all over the world, instantly and constantly, seems normal and natural.

And so, movements of young people all over the world are connected. While we may not be organizing on a specific issue together, we draw inspiration from each other. One of the highlights of the event was a conversation between Oscar Morales (who created the Facebook group One Million Voices Against FARC in 2006, which began the collapse of the Colombian terrorist network FARC) and Wael Ghonim (the Google executive who created a Facebook page called We are All Khaled Said in 2010, which began the Egyptian revolution). The two met at One Young World for the first time, but they'd always been "together." They are members of a generation fighting the same fight, taking advantage of the tools they know so well, offering a fresh approach to long-standing forces in their respective countries. There are hardly any problems today that aren't global problems—from the environment to the economy—our world is becoming more and more interdependent. We can only confront these issues globally and in solidarity, and where our older leaders have failed, millennials are joining hands across the world to step up to the plate.

"*In an era when we must tear down organizational walls, collaborate and share information, this generation has been doing exactly that since they were given group projects in elementary school.*"

The Millennial Generation Holds Great Promise to Radically Improve the US Government

Russ Linden

Russ Linden argues in the following viewpoint that young people today are motivated and eager to bring change to government. Claiming that Millennials have grown up with the tools to connect with others and share information in an effort to problem-solve, Linden maintains that US youth are poised to tear down bureaucracy and remake government in order to make a difference. Linden is a management educator and author. His most recent book is Leading Across Boundaries: Creating Collaborative Agencies in a Networked World.

As you read, consider the following questions:

1. According to the categories established by William Strauss and Neil Howe, to what generational group do the Millennials belong?
2. What are some of the reservations Linden has about Millennials?
3. Why are Millennials so eager to collaborate, according to Linden?

With good reason, Tom Brokaw coined the term "the greatest generation," in his book of the same name, to describe those who grew up during the Great Depression and went on to persevere through WWII. I was raised by two members of this remarkable group and I'm continually astonished by both the accomplishments of their generation and their mental fortitude. These people faced one enormous challenge after another, handled those challenges beautifully and without complaint, and did so with humility and a positive spirit.

It's just possible that we're about to witness another great generation.

That's my take after reading the intriguing book *Generations*, by William Strauss and Neil Howe. The authors identify a pattern of four generations that have repeated sequentially throughout American history since 1584 (the only period in which a generation was skipped was during the Civil War).

Generational Types

The four generational types they discovered are:

Adaptives. They tend to be risk averse, like to conform to existing norms, and try to live up to the high standards of the powerful generation that preceded them. The most recent Adaptive cohort includes those born from 1925–1946.

Idealists. They often inspire a "spiritual awakening." Their strengths include visionary leadership and their shortcomings can include a tendency toward narcissism. The most recent Idealistic cohort was the baby boom generation, born 1946–1964.

Reactives. They tend to be alienated and highly individualistic and are skeptical of existing institutions and of the Idealists who preceded them. The most recent Reactive cohort, commonly referred to as Generation X, was born between 1964 and 1980.

Civics. This group is called an "institution building" generation. Like the Idealists, they tend to set the social agenda for the country. They respect authority, are comfortable working within the system, and set very high goals. The most recent Civic cohort was born between 1980 and 2000.

The Idealist and Civic cohorts are change-oriented generations, the other two reflect a more stable and conservative orientation. The twenty-somethings now entering the workplace are a Civic generation, often referred to as Millennials. And, if you believe Strauss and Howe's premise, they offer enormous promise for our organizations and our society.

What the Next Generation Has to Offer

My wife and I have two adult "Millennial" children. They and their friends reflect most of the characteristics that Civics have historically demonstrated. Moreover, the research on Millennials who are now in the workplace suggests that this group's strengths align beautifully with government's most pressing needs. Consider the following list of traits exhibited by Millennials:

- a great facility for technology
- an eagerness for change
- an assumption that information is to be shared, not hoarded

Millennials' Progressive Attitudes

The political attitudes and policy preferences of Millennials reinforce their liberal self-concept. They are far less likely than their elders and than the other generations when they were young to feel that the government wastes a lot of money. They had more progressive attitudes than the general population on federal aid to schools and were just as likely as the eldest respondents to say that the government should provide universal health insurance. Not only do these positions reflect progressive sentiments, they also are relevant for discussions of a new social contract. . . .

Although people tend to become more conservative as they age and settle into roles (steady job, marriage, family), where they stand in young adulthood is a good barometer of their political views later on. The trends . . . suggest that, as the Millennial replace their elders, we should expect a greater openness to the role of government in providing services and addressing public problems, more confidence in the branches of government, increasing support for the civil liberties of diverse groups, and an increasing identification with service to the community as an integral aspect of personal identity.

Peter Levine, Constance Flanagan, and
Les Gallay, The Millennial Pendulum: A New
Generation of Voters and the Prospects for a
Political Realignment. *Washington, DC: New*
American Foundation, February 2008.

- a lack of patience with bureaucracy
- a talent (and preference) for collaboration
- a passion for service, and
- a desire to make a (big) difference

Wouldn't you want such people working for you?

Yes, this group can be problematic. Their impatience with bureaucracy can get them in trouble, and their expectations for immediate change can leave them easily disappointed. As a result of their early life experiences (e.g., being carted by parents from one structured activity to another) many Millennials need more adult attention and supervision than managers may choose to give. But, consider this group's potential for radically improving government.

Millennials Are Redefining Civic Engagement

At a time when most government agencies need to find new ways to engage their citizen-customers as active partners, Millennials are able and eager to redefine citizen engagement by harnessing the power of Web 2.0. In a "discontinuous" age of incredible global changes, Millennials aren't unsettled by the turbulence; on the contrary, they are energized by it. In an era when we must tear down organizational walls, collaborate and share information, this generation has been doing exactly that since they were given group projects in elementary school (and were graded for how well they worked in a group).

These are all generalizations, of course, and you'll no doubt find many exceptions. But my experience with a number of Millennials tells me that this generation does share the characteristics described in recent research. Moreover, they reflect the fundamental nature of Civic generations discovered by Howe and Strauss.

The next time you're truly despondent about your own team, or division, or agency, just reflect on this fact: most of the Founding Fathers were members of a Civic generation (Jefferson, Madison, Hamilton, Monroe, John Marshall, John Jay and many other Founders were born 1742–1766). The Civics are, indeed, an institution-building generation. The real challenge is ours: Will we be farsighted and smart enough to put today's Civic cohort into appropriate positions of leadership so they can build tomorrow's government?

"*One of the personality traits that distinguish millennials from previous generations is that they gravitate to specific personalities, not institutions or a fixed set of ideals.*"

The Millennial Generation Prefers Collective Problem-Solving over Political Allegiance

David Schimke

In the viewpoint that follows, David Schimke contends that the Millennial generation has been more progressive in its political outlook because it resists timeworn institutions and distrusts factionalism and groups that claim to have all the answers. For these reasons, Schimke claims young people are drawn to politicians who preach inclusiveness and collective problem solving. While he asserts that figures such as President Barack Obama seem to speak this compelling rhetoric, Schimke acknowledges that Millennials are not set in their political ways and could easily be attracted to other strong leaders of any political stripe who convincingly project the inclusive spirit of the young generation. Schimke is the editor in chief of the Utne Reader, *a progressive newsmagazine.*

David Schimke, "Generation Misunderstood," *Utne Reader*, September–October 2009, issue 155, pp. 4–5. Utne.com. Copyright © 2009 by Utne Reader. All rights reserved. Reproduced by permission.

As you read, consider the following questions:

1. According to Schimke, what strategy did liberal politicians adopt after losing the presidency to George W. Bush in 2004?
2. According to Morley Winograd and Michael D. Hais, what percent of eligible voters will Millennials comprise in 2020?
3. Why has President Obama been so successful in courting the Millennial vote, according to Rick Stevens?

In the midst of World War I, French Prime Minister Aristide Briand quipped, "The man who is not a socialist at 20 has no heart, but if he is still a socialist at 40 he has no head." The sentiment, which [former British Prime Minister] Winston Churchill anglicized and made famous, has since been repurposed, retreaded, and quoted as gospel by playwrights, philosophers, political columnists, and my beloved uncle Bob, who once referred to me as "Fidel" after a friendly family debate.

Assuming clichés become clichés for a reason, I had imagined until just a few months ago that early one morning in the not-so-distant future, I'd bolt awake, smash the HD clock radio still on sale at NPR.org, Google the *American Conservative*'s job board, and seek out a meeting of Taxpayers Anonymous. After all, I'm a fortysomething guy from Wisconsin who still attends Green Bay Packer games in 30-below weather. How the hell could I fend off the conservative spirits that lurk in the shadow of death?

A Progressive Generation

Well, as it turns out, Monsieur Briand hadn't done his homework. According to Morley Winograd and Michael D. Hais, authors of *Millennial Makeover: MySpace, YouTube, and the Future of American Politics*, the aging process is more or less apolitical. "While it is true that on certain specific questions people's opinions may change as they gain whatever wisdom comes from experience," the coauthors write, "it is also true that most people rarely change the fundamental patterns of perceptions, beliefs, and attitudes they learn when they are growing up."

I picked up *Millennial Makeover* in mid-July, after returning from the 2009 Campus Progress National Conference in Washington, D.C., where President Bill Clinton and *The Daily Show*'s John Oliver were tasked with firing up 1,000 budding progressives who had gathered to discuss pivotal issues ranging from health care to human rights. The day before the conference, Campus Camp Wellstone hosted a grassroots training session; the day after was set aside for the *Nation*'s Youth Journalism Conference, where I'd been invited to hang out with college-age alternative journalists.

I wish I could have spent more time talking shop with these fledgling storytellers. They had an infectious energy, shot through with self-confidence and optimism. I left the event both inspired by and curious about the millennial generation, born between 1980 and 2001, whom Emory University English professor and author Mark Bauerlein recently disparaged in his widely reviewed book *The Dumbest Generation: How the Digital Age Stupefies Young Americans and Jeopardizes Our Future.*

Bauerlein argues that by de-emphasizing reading and over-emphasizing digital technology, America has produced millions of citizens ignorant of history and unable to analyze the information that's washing over them at warp speed. Ultimately, though, Bauerlein is so seduced by the provocative nature of his argument, he neglects to draw a three-dimensional portrait of his subjects.

Rick Stevens, a journalism professor at the University of Colorado at Boulder who specializes in new media, helped me fill in the holes. He agrees that millennials could stand a few more lessons in media literacy. Still, their innate "BS meters" fascinate him.

"Millennials are immediately suspicious of people who claim to have all the answers," Stevens says. "They don't want platitudes.

When they see problems, they want to work on solutions. They have a more try-and-see mentality. They're more collective."

In February, Russ Linden, an educator who specializes in organizational methodology in the public sector, wrote on Governing's website that millennials have a great facility for technology and an eagerness for change, believe information should be shared, lack patience with bureaucracy, and harbor a passion for service.

"It's possible that we're about to witness another great generation," he says.

Harnessing Technology to Bring Together Young Voters

Conservatives spent the past 20 years perfecting the art of spin, creating an institutionalized echo chamber that some on the left, particularly liberal activists who came of age during the [Ronald] Reagan revolution, are still trying in vain and at their own peril to emulate. After losing to [George W.] Bush in 2004, but learning a great deal from Howard Dean's ability to exploit the Web in early primaries, high-level Democrats like former Clinton chief of staff John Podesta, founder of the Center for American Progress—which runs Campus Progress—encouraged their organizations to hit the computer books. The goal: Harness the untapped power of social media and woo the youth vote.

By any measure, the effort has been a success. Barack Obama won a "stunning 66 percent of voters 18–29" in the 2008 election, Ronald Brownstein reported on *The Atlantic*'s website in May [2009]. At the time of Brownstein's post, President Obama was scoring "positive approval ratings from a dizzying 75 percent of voters under 30."

If Republicans cannot figure out a way to reverse this trend, and quickly, party leaders believe it could prove to be a jackpot for Democrats that pays out for decades. Winograd and Hais calculate that by 2012, 61 percent of the millennials will be eligible to vote, and they'll compose 24 percent of the electorate. In 2016,

Millennials Are Tolerant Freethinkers

Are the kids all right? Not if you listen to some of our leading social commentators. To hear people such as Juliet Schor and William Bennett tell it, today's youth have been virtually brainwashed by marketers, advertisers, and a mushy-headed professoriate. But if your measure of "all right" is a group that is not just tolerant of but welcomes diversity, if it is young adults who do not march in lockstep with any political ideology, who in the majority are willing to think through the subtleties of some of the most contentious issues of the time, if the measure is eighteen- to twenty-nine-year-olds who are open with one another to an astounding degree and take their cues globally, not just locally, then, yes, the kids are doing just fine.

John Zogby, The Way We'll Be: The Zogby Report on the Transformation of the American Dream. New York: Random House, 2008.

they could constitute 30 percent of all eligible voters, in 2020 as much as 36 percent. The data is so promising that in May, John Halpin and Ruy Teixeira, writing for the American Prospect, used it to bolster their conclusion that "new research on ideology refutes the conservative myth that America is a 'center-right' nation."

At the end of their piece, Halpin and Teixeira pull the knockout punch, conceding that "conservatives are not out of the ideological hunt altogether" and acknowledging that voters "are often fickle and prone to significant shifts in opinion." It's a wisely placed asterisk, but fickleness is not part of the equation.

It's just not clear to whom the millennials will ultimately pledge allegiance.

"The political party that will benefit from the coming re-alignment is not preordained," Winograd and Hais point out in *Millennial Makeover*. "The campaigns, candidates, and events of the rest of this decade will determine which party gains the life-long allegiance of this new generation and, with it, a dominant advantage in the next civic era of American politics."

In other words, even in the wake of Obama's ascension, it's way too early for progressives to conclude, as some in the opinion-driven blogosphere already have, that *the kids are alright*. As Brownstein observes, "it is the lasting loyalty of this mammoth young generation . . . that is the real prize at play."

A Strong Personality Speaking to Inclusiveness

It's true, for now, that the Republican Party's loudest members are still running their mouths like it was 1999. But tech-savvy operatives, leveraging the right's considerable financial resources and organizational skills, are playing catch-up behind the scenes. Meanwhile, Democrats have gone a long way in the past eight months to prove [activist and politician] Ralph Nader's thesis that both parties are equally incompetent, corruptible, and out of touch.

What the politicos haven't seemed to grasp yet is that one of the personality traits that distinguish millennials from previous generations is that they gravitate to specific personalities, not institutions or a fixed set of ideals. They will commit, but they have no patience for disingenuousness, a function of the BS meter Rick Stevens refers to. Which is why, in Stevens' opinion, Obama's ability to maintain his pragmatic political posture may be more significant than any single piece of legislation or bit of rhetoric either party chooses to highlight in 2010.

"Obama appeals to [the Millennials] because he's speaking to them in their practical language," Stevens says. "It's a different politic. It's not about left versus right and whoever wins jams stuff down the other's throat. His idea is that everyone can be part of the solution. That's why the younger generation, conservative and liberal, overwhelmingly went for him.

"They are the ultimate generation at being misunderstood. When someone is demonized, they're looking for the other side of the story."

"*Perhaps the biggest impact Millennials will have on the country's religious landscape is to increase its diversity and expand the definition of what faiths are recognized as part of the American mainstream.*"

The Millennial Generation Is Challenging Institutional Religion in America

Morley Winograd and Michael D. Hais

Morley Winograd and Michael D. Hais assert in the following viewpoint that while the Millennial generation in the United States is still committed to spiritual values, it is less inclined to be affiliated with traditional Protestant or Catholic religious institutions. In part, this is due to the growing ethnic diversity of the United States, bringing more Hindus, Buddhists, and Muslims into the cultural mix, the authors contend. However, Winograd and Hais also claim that the lack of affiliation with dogmatic religions has much to do with Millennials tolerance for traditionally-polarizing issues such as gay rights and evolutionary biology that are often condemned by institutional religion. In the end, Winograd and Hais maintain that the religious denominations that will likely attract the most Millennials are those that stress public service and inclusiveness, two important ideals shared by many of today's youth. Winograd and Hais are coauthors of Millennial Momentum: How a New Generation is Remaking America *and* Millennial Makeover: MySpace, YouTube, and the Future of American Politics. *Both are members of NDN, a progressive think tank that analyzes issues of political, economic, and technological change in a globalized world.*

As you read, consider the following questions:

1. As Winograd and Hais claim, what percent of Millennials has left the religious denomination of their childhood?
2. As the authors report, what percent of Millennials define themselves as Christian? What percent of older Americans consider themselves Christian?
3. According to Winograd and Hais, what do generational theorists think the religious outlook of the children and grandchildren of Millennials will be?

While most religions believe their doctrines and practices to be eternal verities, all denominations, like other institutions, must continually enlist and renew the commitment of each new generation if they are to survive and carry on their work. At perhaps no other time in the nation's history has this task been more challenging for America's religious faiths than it is now.

It is not that the country's newest generation of young adults, the Millennial Generation, rejects the spiritual values that deeply permeate the nation's culture.

Americans, to a greater extent than those who live in other Western countries, believe in God (in numbers ranging from two-thirds to 80 percent depending on how pollsters ask the question). Millennials, born in the years 1982 through 2003, fully share this belief with older generations, according to the

173

Pew Research Center. Two-thirds of Millennials (64 percent) are certain God exists.

Many Millennials Are Unaffiliated with Religious Denominations

In spite of these beliefs, however, a large majority of Millennials (72 percent) describe themselves as "more spiritual than religious," according to a LiteWay Christian Resources survey.

Millennials are significantly less likely than older Americans to be members of a specific denomination or to participate in traditional religious rituals. About 1 in 5 Millennials (18 percent) has left the denomination of their childhood and a quarter of them are completely unaffiliated with any denomination. Millennials are also less likely than older generations to attend religious services weekly or to read Scripture, pray, and meditate regularly.

And for any who may believe that the generation's lesser commitment to specific denominations or participation in religious rituals simply stems from youthful skepticism, Pew tracking surveys indicate otherwise. Millennials are twice as likely to be unaffiliated with a specific denomination than were baby boomers in the 1970s and 1½ times more likely than were members of Generation X in the 1990s—when both of those cohorts were the age that Millennials are today.

Recognizing and Respecting Diversity

In the end, however, perhaps the biggest impact Millennials will have on the country's religious landscape is to increase its diversity and expand the definition of what faiths are recognized as part of the American mainstream.

Since ratification in 1791, the First Amendment has protected the rights of religious minorities and nonbelievers. But from the beginning, the United States has been predominantly a Christian, and more specifically, a Protestant, nation. The Millennials put a large dent in that description.

Millennials Say They Are More Spiritual than Religious

How much would you agree or disagree with this statement: I am more spiritual than religious.

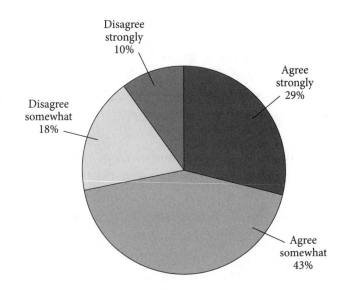

Disagree strongly
10%

Disagree somewhat
18%

Agree strongly
29%

Agree somewhat
43%

TAKEN FROM: Lifeway Research Survey, "American Millennials Are Spiritually Diverse," August 2009.

This generation is not only the most ethnically diverse in US history, it is also the most religiously diverse. Millennials are half as likely to be white Evangelicals or Roman Catholics and a quarter less likely to be white mainline Protestants compared with older generations. By contrast, they are twice as likely to be Hispanic Catholics or unaffiliated and a third more likely to be non-Christians (Jews, Muslims, Hindus, and Buddhists), finds Pew.

As a result of all these trends, only two-thirds (68 percent) of Millennials are Christian, compared with about 80 percent of older Americans. Fewer than half (43 percent) are Protestant, in contrast to 53 percent of all older generations and almost two-thirds of senior citizens.

The nation's religious diversity is likely to increase even more in coming years as ever greater numbers choose spouses across denominational lines. The percentage of mixed-faith marriages rose from 15 percent in 1988 to 25 percent in 2006.

Millennials are particularly willing to cross denominational boundaries in selecting a life partner. In a 2010 survey, less than a quarter of 18-to-23-year-olds thought it was important to marry someone of the same faith. How might America's religious denominations respond to this less ritualistic and more diverse future?

For religious faiths that are thousands of years old, it may make long-term sense to be comforted by the lesson offered in Ecclesiastes, as amplified in the boomer anthems of Simon & Garfunkel and the Byrds: "To everything there is a season, and a time to every purpose under the heaven."

Those who study generations say that American history is cyclical rather than linear. In about four decades a new, young generation of the archetype labeled Idealist by generational theorists will emerge into adulthood. The members of this new cohort—the children and grandchildren of Millennials—will, like today's boomers, be driven by their deeply held internal values, among which traditional religion and its rituals are likely to be very important.

A Commitment to Issues Beyond the Spiritual

In the immediate future, however, religious organizations will have to emphasize those aspects of their belief structures that most strongly mesh with Millennial values.

On one level this means that America's denominations will at least have to recognize that Millennials are far less driven than older generations by traditional beliefs on the cultural issues—

women's rights, homosexuality, and evolution—that have divided the nation since the 1960s.

Millennials will also be drawn by appeals that emphasize service more than doctrine and ritual. No generation in American history has been as involved in national and community service as the Millennial Generation. Millennials make up a disproportionately large and growing share of large national service organizations—the Peace Corps and AmeriCorps, as well as the armed forces.

According to the Corporation for National and Community Service, two-thirds of all youthful community service work is done through nonprofit educational and religious institutions. This faith-based community service participation lets Millennials live their spiritual beliefs in a very basic way and on their own terms. It may also help America's religious denominations weather and perhaps even thrive in the Millennial era ahead.

> *"Many millennials reject the*
> *assumptions of 1960s liberationists in*
> *favor of something more substantial:*
> *the creeds, practices and moral codes*
> *that defined religious life for centuries."*

The Millennial Generation Is Embracing Religion and Its Orthodoxy

Anna Williams

Anna Williams is an editorial intern at USA Today. *In the following viewpoint, she reports that although many young people have shown indifference to traditional religion, a growing number are returning to institutional faiths and drawing inspiration from their liturgies. According to Williams, the Millennial generation has largely discovered that their "liberated" Baby Boom parents and grandparents struggled through an amoral wilderness that promised freedom but provided only self-centered hedonism and social decay. To counteract this sense of purposelessness, Millennials are embracing age-old truths that emphasize communal works and personal fulfillment, Williams writes. Thus, young people are following their faiths, Williams believes, because they want to change the world for the better.*

As you read, consider the following questions:
1. According to Sister Mary Bendyna, why are Millennial Catholics attracted to the lifestyle of priests and nuns?
2. What was the "new creed" that Williams says developed over the latter part of the twentieth century and mired people in a spiritually empty way of life?
3. In Williams' view, what is the demanding yet compelling pull of religious orthodoxy?

Crowds of young people throng the streets, singing, dancing and waving flags from around the world.

When a diminutive figure emerges in a white car, they erupt, jockeying for the best view of this international superstar. A rock idol? A marquee athlete? A political prodigy?

Nope: an old man—more scholar than celebrity—smiling shyly to acknowledge the adulation.

Pope Benedict XVI will arrive this week [in August 2011] in Madrid for a weeklong celebration marked by up to a million teenage and twentysomething Catholics as World Youth Day. The international event gives young Catholics a chance to learn about and practice their faith together: Think Mass, lectures, prayer and more Mass.

But this is not your average religious conference. The music is loud; the hours, late; the attendees, young, diverse, exuberant.

The whole spectacle might understandably confuse those outside of the church: Why would these young people belong to, much less celebrate, such a backward, oppressive institution as the Roman Catholic Church? And why do they seem to find Pope Benedict, 84, not just endearing but also inspiring? The answers to these questions lie in the discontent and desires of a peculiar subset of the millennial generation.

A Resurgence of Traditional Religion Among the Young

At first glance, studies such as Pew's 2010 report "Religion Among the Millennials" seem to indicate that young Catholics (age 18–29) exemplify their generation's tendency toward religious indifference. To wit, they are less likely to attend Mass weekly, less likely to pray daily, and less likely to consider religion "very important" than Catholics 30 and older. Yet the millennial Catholics who do practice and value their faith are doing something odd: They are spearheading a resurgence of traditional Catholic liturgy and disciplines that their parents and grandparents had largely abandoned.

A recent study of Catholic religious orders confirmed this trend. Sister Mary Bendyna, a member of the Sisters of Mercy of the Americas and director of the Georgetown University-affiliated center that conducted the study, summarized the findings for the *New York Times*. Compared with older generations, she said, millennials who consider becoming priests or nuns are "more attracted to a traditional style of religious life, where there is community living, common prayer, having Mass together, praying the Liturgy of the Hours (the church's daily cycle of Scripture readings and prayers) together."

"They are much more likely to say fidelity to the church is important to them," she added. "And they really are looking for communities where members wear habits," the age-old garb of monks and nuns.

A similar desire for traditional religious practice has developed in recent years among many young Protestants, Jews and Muslims, according to a 2007 analysis by the *U.S. News and World Report*. Evangelical Christians, for example, are reciting the Nicene Creed, a fourth century expression of Christian doctrine, and offering weekly Communion services, while some once dismissed both practices as remnants of ritualistic and spiritually dead Catholicism. Jews—and not only Orthodox Jews— are obeying dietary and religious laws more closely and using more Hebrew in synagogues. Muslims are more strictly embracing the Islamic calendar of prayer and fasting. This surprising cross-denominational trend raises a broader question: What attracts today's youth to such "old-fashioned" orthodoxy?

The Search for Fulfillment and Harmony

As a member of this strange millennial cohort, I have wondered this myself. I think the answer comes down to this: 1960s-style liberation—from moral codes, family obligations, religious commitments—has betrayed us.

Sometime in the past century, a new creed emerged, saying everyone should make his own creed. This tolerant, open-minded ethos seemed to promise freedom: safe sex with many partners, drugs and alcohol galore and quick, no-fault divorce. So our Baby Boomer parents partied hard, yet in so many cases left us only the hangover: heartbreak, addiction and broken homes, plus rising rates of teenage depression and suicide.

The anything-goes religion of the late 20th century cannot prevent nor even explain these consequences. (After all, if I'm OK, you're OK, and we can do whatever we want, why are so many people unhappy?) When every member of a society does whatever makes him feel good, the inevitable results are not personal fulfillment and communal harmony but selfishness and social breakdown.

With these realizations in mind, many millennials reject the assumptions of 1960s liberationists in favor of something more substantial: the creeds, practices and moral codes that defined religious life for centuries. Unlike reductionistic scientism or vague romanticism, traditional religions propose specific, compelling explanations for the world in front of us—broken, fraught with suffering, enslaved to sin, but nonetheless revealing glimpses of beauty and greatness.

More intellectually coherent than relativism, orthodoxy is also more demanding. It makes us place others above ourselves, the truth above what we'd like to be true, the fight for virtue above the pursuit of pleasure. In a word, it preaches sacrifice.

A Mission to Change the World

These themes will be prominent in Madrid this week, as Catholics of all nationalities gather for prayer and festivity. So why are they happy to be Catholic? Because they have concluded that the church's teachings are, in fact, true, and because they've recognized that true freedom lies in self-sacrifice. Far from repressive, such realizations are—as millennials of other faiths can attest—thrilling.

Pope Benedict knows that young people ponder these matters and desire more than what today's culture offers. When he speaks to them, he doesn't water it down. His voice is quiet, even gentle, but he's not afraid to challenge his congregation. And he is right to do so: Young people don't need another meaningless affirmation of their worth. They want an explanation of how the world is and a mission that involves changing it. Their question is no longer, "What will make me feel good?" but "What will make me a good person, and how can I do good for the world?"

Whatever you believe, you have to admit: They're asking the right questions.

"The growing support for gay and lesbian rights, driven in large part by the millennial generation, makes it likely that we will look back on 2011 as the year marking a sea change in views on gay and lesbian issues that will change politics on both sides of the aisle."

The Millennial Generation Is More Accepting of Gay and Lesbian Rights

Robert P. Jones

Robert P. Jones is the CEO of the Public Religion Research Institute, a nonpartisan research organization that contends with issues of religion and public life. Jones is also a blog columnist on the Washington Post website. In the following viewpoint, he reports that the Millennial generation is largely in support for homosexual rights such as same-sex marriage and adoption of children by gay and lesbian couples. For Jones, this support is changing the political and religious landscape on these issues because a large number of young people of all political stripes and of various denominations favor an acceptance of gay rights. Jones even claims that 2011 may be the watershed year in which attitudes in the United States toward same-sex marriage and gay adoption reveal majority approval.

As you read, consider the following questions:

1. According to Jones's Public Religion Research Institute poll, what percent of Millennials favor gay and lesbian marriage?
2. Since what year has same-sex marriage received double-digit increases in public support, according to Jones?
3. What percent of white mainline Protestants now support same-sex marriage, as reported by the Religion Research Institute poll?

Over a week ago, [governor of Texas and 2012 Republican presidential hopeful] Rick Perry added his name to the National Organization for Marriage's pledge to support a federal marriage amendment defining marriage as between a man and a woman, bringing the number of GOP presidential candidates who have signed on to the pledge to four. Although Perry's previous declaration that states should have the ultimate say on the issue of same-sex marriage has netted him some accusations of hypocrisy, the move to declare his backing for a constitutional amendment may seem unavoidable if Perry is to compete for evangelical Protestant and tea party votes, two groups that are strongly opposed to same-sex marriage.

A Generation Gap on Gay and Lesbian Issues

New data from the Public Religion Research Institute shows, however, that this Republican campaign dynamic—opposition to same-sex marriage as a litmus test of conservative authenticity—has waning appeal to younger Republicans now, and promises to lose steam in years to come. Our new poll, "Millennials, Religion and Gay & Lesbian Issues," released on August 29, [2011] shows

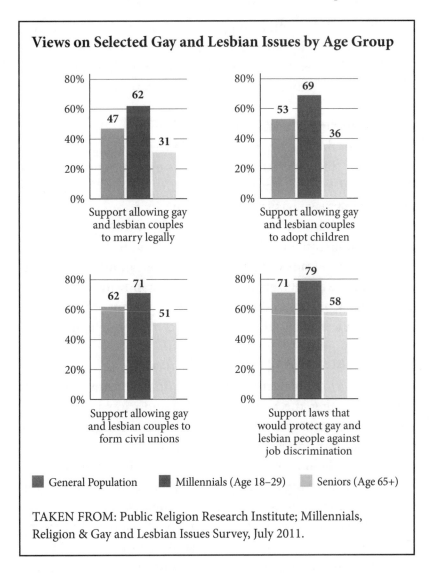

Views on Selected Gay and Lesbian Issues by Age Group

Support allowing gay
and lesbian couples
to marry legally

Support allowing gay
and lesbian couples
to adopt children

Support allowing gay
and lesbian couples to
form civil unions

Support laws that
would protect gay and
lesbian people against
job discrimination

■ General Population ■ Millennials (Age 18–29) ▢ Seniors (Age 65+)

TAKEN FROM: Public Religion Research Institute; Millennials,
Religion & Gay and Lesbian Issues Survey, July 2011.

a 20-point generation gap between millennials (age 18 to 29)
and seniors (age 65 and up) on a whole range of gay and lesbian
issues.

On the more contested issues of same-sex marriage and
adoption of children by gay and lesbian couples, millennials are
approximately twice as likely as seniors to support them. While

only about 1-in-3 seniors support same-sex marriage (31 percent) or adoption by gay and lesbian couples (36 percent), more than 6-in-10 millennials support both issues, with 62 percent favoring gay and lesbian marriage, and 69 percent in support of gay adoption.

These findings are arresting, not only for what they say about the future of these issues in political debates in the general public, because this generation gap persists even among conservative political and religious groups. Public support for allowing same-sex marriage has seen double-digit increases over the past five years, a dramatic shift in public opinion that appears to be carrying along millennial Republicans with it. Just under half of younger Republicans (49 percent of Republican millennials and 44 percent of Republicans ages 30–44) favor allowing gay and lesbian people to marry, compared to only 19 percent of Republican seniors and less than one-third (31 percent) of all Republicans.[1]

Denominations Are Split on the Issues

The survey also uncovered another shifting dynamic that will increasingly alter the political calculus and campaign strategy. Politicians have long assumed that the battle lines over same-sex marriage are drawn between secular Americans who support it and religious Americans who oppose it. But millennials are also transforming the religious landscape, and there are now major religious groups on both sides of these debates. Majorities of non-Christian religiously affiliated Americans (67 percent), Catholics (52 percent), and white mainline Protestants (51 percent) favor allowing gay and lesbian couples to marry. On the other hand, 6-in-10 (60 percent) African American Protestants and approximately three-quarters (76 percent) of white evangelical Protestants oppose allowing gay and lesbian couples to marry.

Cultural transformations are always difficult to discern on their leading edge, and there is always the possibility that unforeseen future events may alter even strong trends. But it is notable, for example, that 2011 is the first year that supporting same-sex marriage is not a minority position. The growing support for gay and lesbian rights, driven in large part by the millennial generation, makes it likely that we will look back on 2011 as the year marking a sea change in views on gay and lesbian issues that will change politics on both sides of the aisle.

Note

1. The analysis of millennial Republicans is based on less than 100 cases (N=85). Some caution should be exercised in interpreting these results.

Periodical Bibliography

The following articles have been selected to supplement the diverse views presented in this chapter.

Ronald Brownstein   "Millennial Tremors," *National Journal*, February 14, 2009.

James Fallows   "Millennials' Uncertain Future," *National Journal*, May 8, 2010.

Bradley N. Hill   "Missing the Signs," *Christian Century*, April 5, 2011.

Jamie L. Manson   "A New Generation, a New Kind of Leadership," *National Catholic Reporter*, October 28, 2011.

Monica Martinez   "Students as Smart Mobs," *Phi Delta Kappan*, September 2009.

Lauren McKayn   "Generation Green: Why Gen Y and the Millennials Are Greener than You'll Ever Be," *CRM Magazine*, April 2010.

Stephen Prothero   "Is Religion Losing the Millennial Generation?," *USA Today*, February 4, 2008.

Carla Seaquist   "Hope for Reversing America's Decline: the Millennial Generation," *Christian Science Monitor*, September 24, 2010.

Eric Utne   "Let's Get On with It," *Utne Reader*, March–April 2009.

Morley Winograd and Michael D. Hais   "Occupy Movement Mirrors Millennial Generation," *Christian Science Monitor*, October 27, 2011.

For Further Discussion

Chapter 1

1. Steve Chapman and David N. Bass both quote researcher Jean Twenge, but each makes contrasting statements about the traits of the current young generation. Chapman identifies himself as a member of an older generation and Bass identifies himself as a member of the current, younger generation. How does this self-definition influence your agreement or disagreement with their views? Keeping in mind each author's association with a different generation, which viewpoint do you find more convincing and why?

2. In John Palfrey's and Urs Gasser's view, the millennial generation is comprised of digital natives; however, Chris Jones and Laura Czerniewicz do not believe digital natives and immigrants are divided along generational lines alone. Consider you and your friends' status as digital natives. Does this term, as defined by Palfrey and Gasser apply to you? Now consider your parents and older people you know. Are they strictly digital immigrants, or do some of those people cross the divide and act more like digital natives? In the end, decide whether you think digital natives is a strictly generational term using your personal observations as evidence to support your claim.

3. Do you think that David N. Bass makes a valid argument that the current young generation lacks a strong work ethic and doesn't understand the demands of real life? Do you agree with Brynn Evans' argument that the work practices of young workers offer many benefits to their employers? Finally, do you believe, as Rick Jensen does, that these work practices will lead to more entrepreneurship than in the past? Support your answers with both your own examples and quotes from the viewpoints.

Chapter 2

1. The first two viewpoints in Chapter Two address the motivation and intelligence of the Millennial generation. As a student, which one of these viewpoints paints a more accurate picture of student life today? Do you think Jayson's portrait of the overworked student more truthfully defines you and your classmates, or does Bauerlein provide a more correct assessment? Give examples to support your view.

2. Much discussion in education today revolves around the incorporation of digital technologies. After reading the viewpoint by Prensky, conduct some additional research into the subject. Do you think the incorporation of additional technologies into the classroom would enhance education? Is there still a place for old modes of education? Use quotes from the viewpoint and any articles you find to support your view.

3. When reading Singham's viewpoint on generational stereotyping, did you feel that your teachers have stereotyped you? Have you ever been guilty of stereotyping your teachers for being outside of your generation? How can this gap between generations be bridged to improve education? Use your experiences as well as quotes from the viewpoint to support your claims.

Chapter 3

1. According to Mitchell E. Daniels Jr., what problems have the Baby Boom generation handed down to the Millennials? How does Stephen Moore refute Daniels's argument? Why does he claim that the Millennial generation is ungrateful to the Boomers? Do you think the Millennial generation owes a debt of thanks to Baby Boomers, or should it be justly resentful of the Boomers' legacy? Explain why.

2. Eleni Towns contends that the terrorist attacks of September 11, 2001, have significantly impacted the lives of the

Millennial generation and continue to influence their behavior and attitudes. Joan Garrett, however, claims that, while a momentous event, the 9/11 attacks have lost much of their influence over the daily lives of young people. With whose opinion do you agree? What evidence—either from within the viewpoints or from your own experience—has led you to side with either Towns or Garrett? Explain your answer.

Chapter 4

1. David D. Burstein and Russ Linden see the Millennial generation as a great force of change in the United States and the world. Reread these viewpoints and explain which arguments you agree or disagree with. Do you believe the Millennial generation is poised to remake the nation and the world, or is this forecast too optimistic? Support your answer with evidence from the viewpoints or from other sources.

2. Morley Winograd and Michael D. Hais claim that statistical evidence reveals that young people in the United States are less affiliated with traditional, institutional religion than past generations. They insist that those Millennials who define themselves as spiritual are more attracted to progressive denominations that stress tolerance and inclusiveness, two values the generation supposedly embraces. Anna Williams maintains, however, that many Millennials are returning to traditional religions because these institutions offer strong values that stand against the relativism and spiritual emptiness that mired previous generations. Using the evidence in these viewpoints, critique the strengths and weaknesses of both arguments. Whose opinion do you agree with, or is there another way to view the role and significance of religion for this generation? Explain.

3. Choose the three legacies for which you think the Millennial generation will be most remembered. Using evidence from

the viewpoints, explain why and how you made your selections. In answering the question, describe what impact these three legacies are likely to have on the world and future generations.

Organizations to Contact

The editors have compiled the following list of organizations con-
cerned with the issues debated in this book. The descriptions are
derived from materials provided by the organizations. All have
publications or information available for interested readers. The
list was compiled on the date of publication of the present volume;
the information provided here may change. Be aware that many
organizations take several weeks or longer to respond to inquiries,
so allow as much time as possible.

Brookings Institute
1775 Massachusetts Avenue NW
Washington, DC 20036
(202) 797-6000
website: www.brookings.edu

The Brookings Institute is a nonprofit research institute dedicated to carrying out reliable research that provides a basis for
policy suggestions to improve the US democracy; ensure economic and social welfare, security, and opportunity for the citizens of the country; and create an international system based
on security, prosperity, and cooperation. Recent research and
commentary from the organization has focused on how the
Millennial generation will influence these goals. Articles including "Millennial Generation: The Next Big Thing," "What Does
the Next Generation of American Leaders Think?," and "Where
Today's Youth Actually Get Their News" can all be read on the
Brookings website.

Center for American Progress (CAP)
1333 H Street NW, 10th Floor
Washington, DC 20005
(202) 682-1611 • fax (202) 682-1867
website: www.americanprogress.org

CAP is a public policy organization that advocates for the implementation of progressive ideas and action that will help Americans live better lives. In order to achieve this goal, the organization seeks to change public policy, counter conservative policy, push the media to address issues of national importance, and frame public debate on pertinent issues. While the center's work covers a wide range of topics, recent research has been dedicated to the shift occurring in US society as a result of the Millennial generation's advance into prominence. Articles such as "The Progressive Generation: How Young Americans View Economic Issues and Why It Matters," and "The Generation Gap on Government" detail this generation's views.

Center for Information and Research on Civic Learning and Engagement (CIRCLE)

Jonathan M. Tisch College of Citizenship and Public Service
Lincoln Filene Hall
Tufts University
Medford, MA 02155
(617) 627-4710 • fax (617) 627-3401
e-mail: civicyouth@tufts.edu
website: www.civicyouth.org

Since 2001 CIRCLE has been conducting research focused on the civic engagement of US youth from their education to their political participation. With the development of research in this field, the center has influenced the discussion about the young generation of citizens, encouraged politics to include these citizens in political campaigns, and helped train organizations on how to reach young Americans. A wide range of topics including civic knowledge, concepts of citizenship, and civic education have been researched extensively with findings and reports available on the CIRCLE website.

Generation 18

e-mail: info@generation18.com
website: www.generation18.com

Generation 18 formed prior to the 2008 presidential election with the goal of registering, engaging, and mobilizing young voters. Since that election, the organization has continued to use film and media to encourage these voters' participation in the political sphere. Videos documenting the project's efforts can be viewed online along with founder David D. Burstein's blog, which provides many articles documenting the Millennial generation's impact on society.

Generations United

1331 H Street NW, Suite 900
Washington, DC 20005
(202) 289-3979
website: www.gu.org

A membership organization comprised of more than one hundred organizations representing Americans at the national, state, and local levels, Generations United seeks to foster intergenerational cooperation and strategies to ensure children, youth, and older people live fulfilled and productive lives as US citizens. The groups' work includes public policy advocacy as well as more focused work on issues faced by multigenerational families.

Mobilize.org

1875 K Street NW, 5th Floor
Washington, DC 20006
(202) 642-4320
e-mail: info@mobilize.org
website: www.mobilize.org

Mobilize.org seeks to find lasting solutions to the most challenging problems facing today's generation of youth by engaging these individuals in the solution process. One of the main vehicles to foster this engagement is the Democracy 2.0 Summit. During these gatherings, Millennials work together to address issues such as financial literacy, money and politics, Millennial veterans, and education. Details about these conferences can be found on the Mobilize.org website. Additionally, the Millennial Report Blog provides a forum for Millennials to post about issues they face today.

National Education Association (NEA)

1201 16th Street NW
Washington, DC 20036-3290
(202) 833-4000 • fax (202) 822-7974
website: www.nea.org

NEA works to ensure that all US children have access to a quality public education. Its focus ranges from federal legislative issues to local school policy level issues. NEA's website and magazine feature articles such as "Humor and the Net Generation" addressing the implementation of new technologies in the classroom.

National Youth Leadership Council (NYLC)

1667 Snelling Avenue North, Suite D300
Saint Paul, MN 55108
(851) 631-3672 • fax (651) 631-2955
website: www.nylc.org

NYLC has been working for more than twenty-five years to connect youth, educators, and communities to create a service-learning movement that helps youth move beyond only receiving information to becoming active participants in the democracy. NYLC seeks to carry out its mission through a wide range of projects focusing on everything from service-learning in schools, to leadership, to HIV/AIDS prevention. Information on these projects as well as access to the organization's quarterly publication *The Generator* can be found on the NYLC website.

United States Student Association (USSA)

1211 Connecticut Avenue NW, Suite 406
Washington, DC 20036
(202) 640-6570 • fax (202) 223-4005
e-mail: usaa@usstudents.org
website: www.usstudents.org

USSA was founded in 1947 to provide a voice for US students and youth in the US government. This student-led organization works with government at the local, state, and national levels to ensure that all Americans have the opportunity to receive an education. USSA's work includes legislative advocacy, trainings, and conferences to ensure US youth are always ready to contribute to the national debate on education issues and individual projects dedicated to helping students of color and LGBT students.

Youth and Media

23 Everett Street, Second Floor
Cambridge, MA 02138
(617) 495-7547 • fax (617) 495-7641
e-mail: youthandmedia@cyber.law.harvard.edu
website: www.youthandmedia.org

Youth and Media is a project led by law professors John Palfrey and Urs Gasser at the Berkman Center for Internet & Society at Harvard University. It seeks to develop a better understanding of the interactions between today's younger generation and digital media, address the issues raised by this interaction, utilize this generation's digital fluency in ways that benefit society, and create new regulatory and education guidelines in response to these technologies. The Youth and Media website provides papers and videos addressing these issues.

Youth Service America (YSA)

1101 15th Street NW, Suite 200
Washington, DC 20005

(202) 296-2992 • fax (202) 296-4030
website: www.ysa.org

YSA is an organization that encourages youth participation in civics and politics within their community, believing that engagement with the younger generation is necessary to address the most pressing issues faced by society today. To advance this mission, YSA fosters youth volunteering, academic achievement, and leadership.

Bibliography of Books

Ron Alsop   *The Trophy Kids Grow Up: How
                          the Millennial Generation is
                          Shaking up the Workplace.* San
                          Francisco: Jossey-Bass, 2008.

Mark Bauerlein   *The Digital Divide: Arguments
                          for and Against Facebook, Google,
                          Texting, and the Age of Social
                          Networking.* New York: Jeremy P.
                          Tarcher/Penguin, 2011.

Mark Bauerlein   *The Dumbest Generation: How
                          the Digital Age Stupefies Young
                          Americans and Jeopardizes Our
                          Future (Or, Don't Trust Anyone
                          Under 30).* New York: Jeremy P.
                          Tarcher/Penguin, 2008.

Eric Greenberg with   *Generation We: How Millennial
Karl Weber   Youth Are Taking Over America
                          And Changing Our World Forever.*
                          Emeryville, CA: Pachatusan,
                          2008.

Neil Howe and   *Millennials Rising: The Next Great
William Strauss   Generation.* New York: Vintage,
                          2000.

Rebecca Huntley   *The World According to Y: Inside
                          the New Adult Generation.*
                          Australia: Allen & Unwin, 2006.

Andrew Keen	*The Cult of the Amateur: How Blogs, MySpace, YouTube, and the Rest of Today's User-Generated Media Are Destroying Our Economy, Our Culture, and Our Values.* New York: Doubleday, 2007.
Lynne C. Lancaster and David Stillman	*The M-Factor: How the Millennial Generation Is Rocking the Workplace.* New York: HarperCollins, 2010.
Roger McHaney	*The New Digital Shoreline: How Web 2.0 and Millennials Are Revolutionizing Higher Education.* Sterling, VA: Stylus, 2011.
Michael McQueen	*The New Rules of Engagement: A Guide to Understanding & Connecting With Generation Y.* Garden City, NY: Morgan James, 2010.
John Palfrey and Urs Gasser	*Born Digital: Understanding the First Generation of Digital Natives.* New York: Basic, 2008.
Thom S. Rainer and Jess W. Rainer	*The Millennials: Connecting to America's Largest Generation.* Nashville: B & H Publishing, 2011.
Joanne G. Sujansky and Jan Ferri-Reed	*Keeping the Millennials: Why Companies Are Losing Billions in Turnover to This Generation—and What to Do About It.* Hoboken, NJ: John Wiley & Sons, 2009.

Don Tapscott	*Grown up Digital: How the Net Generation Is Changing Your World.* New York: McGraw-Hill, 2009.
Bruce Tulgan	*Not Everyone Gets a Trophy: How to Manage Generation Y.* San Francisco: Jossey-Bass, 2009.
Sherry Turkle	*Alone Together: Why We Expect More from Technology and Less from Each Other.* New York: Basic, 2011.
Jean M. Twenge	*Generation Me: Why Today's Young Americans Are More Confident, Assertive, Entitled— and More Miserable than Ever Before.* New York: Free Press, 2006.
Jean M. Twenge and W. Keith Campbell	*The Narcissism Epidemic: Living in the Age of Entitlement.* New York: Free Press, 2009.
Dave Verhaagen	*Parenting the Millennial Generation: Guiding Our Children Born Between 1982 and 2000.* Westport, CT: Praeger, 2005.
Morley Winograd and Michael D. Hais	*Millennial Makeover: MySpace, YouTube, and the Future of American Politics.* Piscataway, NJ: Rutgers University Press, 2009.
Morley Winograd and Michael D. Hais	*Millennial Momentum: How a New Generation Is Remaking America.* Piscataway, NJ: Rutgers University Press, 2011.

Kit Yarrow and Jayne O'Donnell

Gen BuY: How Tweens, Teens and Twenty-Somethings Are Revolutionizing Retail. San Francisco: Jossey-Bass, 2009.

Index